Using Data to Make Better Educational Decisions

Philip A. Streifer

The Scarecrow Press, Inc.
A Scarecrow Education book published
with the American Association
of School Administrators
Lanham, Maryland, and London
2002

SCARECROW PRESS, INC.
A ScarecrowEducation Book

Published in the United States of America
by Scarecrow Press, Inc.
4720 Boston Way, Lanham, Maryland 20706
www.scarecroweducation.com

4 Pleydell Gardens, Folkstone
Kent CT20 2DN, England

British Library Cataloguing in Publication Information Available

Library of Congress Cataloging-in-Publication Data

Streifer, Philip Alan.
  Using data to make better educational decisions / Philip A. Streifer.
    p. cm.
  "A Scarecrow Education book published with the American Association of
School Administrators."
  Includes bibliographical references and index.
  ISBN 0-8108-4214-9 (pbk. : alk. paper)
  1. School management and organization—United States—Data processing.
I. Title.
  LB2806.17 .S87 2002
  371.2'00973—dc21   2001049893

∞™ The paper used in this publication meets the minimum requirements of
American National Standard for Information Sciences—Permanence of
Paper for Printed Library Materials, ANSI/NISO Z39.48-1992.
Manufactured in the United States of America.

~

Contents

Introduction

"Hartford Schools Show Progress"[1] read the headline. For years the Hartford, Connecticut, public schools' student achievement scores were abysmal, with little or no progress to show for all their efforts. Recently their new superintendent placed a high priority on data-driven decision-making guided by a host of research-driven strategies and programs known to improve student achievement when properly implemented. As part of their strategy, The CT Academy for Education in Mathematics, Science, and Technology provided each Hartford school with a consolidated bar graph displaying mathematics achievement data on each of thirty math objectives tested over a five-year period. The CT Academy hired a data warehousing company to write the computer code that would quickly and easily extract key data elements from the voluminous state-provided data files and display those data in easy-to-read and understandable graphs. Using these data to benchmark performance and drive instruction (accompanied by a host of instructional strategies), the superintendent, board, staff, teachers, and administrators all worked to improve student learning. In just under six months their efforts appeared to pay off, with significant improvements in student achievement reported. *EdWeek* noted, "In fact, the district improved more in 1999 in mathematics and reading than in the previous four years combined."

The Hartford story is an example where new technologies and techniques can be applied to an old and frustrating problem. While district personnel had access to these data for years, they were in stacks of reports or difficult-to-use computer files. The bar graphs were only part of Hartford's improvement story, as the district conducted many interventions on almost every level—"He [the superintendent] brought with him a toolbox crammed with curricular programs and teaching strategies."[2] But by using clearly presented data delivered in an easy to use format, interventions and improvement strategies were easier to target and implement. The purpose of this book is to explore various examples of how data such as these can be collected, analyzed, presented, and used for school improvement.

Greater advances in data management lie ahead for educators as we begin to fully use information technologies that have been used in the private sector for many years. Business and industry, and in many cases government, fully entered the information age in the 1970s and 1980s. As education enters the twenty-first century, the proliferation of information technologies will enable immediate access to vast amounts of our "corporate" data from which decisions can be made more quickly and easily. Internets, intranets, data warehouses, data marts and repositories, relational databases, satellite linkages, instantaneous data access through cellular phones, world-wide protected networks—all have grown up in the last ten years in response to the private sector's need for real-time, 24×7 (a reference to 24 hours a day, 7 days a week) comprehensive data access to address "mission critical" business decisions. In fact, many global corporations have gone so high-tech that the corporate office has become a thing of the past—rendered unnecessary.

Today's mobile executives rely on laptops that plug into secure corporate networks that can be accessed from literally anywhere in the world. A colleague ran a mid-sized company that specializes in worldwide, wireless data transmission enabling users to receive and type email messages effortlessly on a device no larger than a small pad—all with a two-week battery life! The device eliminates the need for a laptop as large amounts of data can be downloaded quickly and read on its fairly large screen. For the general public, new palm-held devices and digital cellular phones now provide wireless access to the World Wide Web and email (although data entry is still challenging on these devices). Thus, should the need arise to physically go to corporate headquarters or one of the district offices, executives now sign up for cubicles called "touchdown spaces"—spaces to sit down, plug in, and get work done quickly and efficiently. Meetings are held whenever possible via the Internet with tools that facilitate this process or through video conferencing. Several Web-based, Internet conferencing sites are now commercially available to hold meetings and run live demonstrations of software applications or display presentations and the like. As we look to the future we can expect that educators' abilities to use data for decision-making will only be strengthened by using these exciting new technologies. The Hartford story and those that follow are examples I have experienced where new techniques and technologies, coupled with effective leadership practices, have yielded surprising success.

Corporate America has been doing "data-driven decision-making" for decades now, yet this is an emerging field of practice for school leadership. Thus, a further purpose of this book is to promote improved decision-making in schools by applying many of the processes developed in the private sector to our well-established practices of program evaluation and school improvement. For example, with new information technologies we may be able to apply "case-based" and "rule-based" decision-making that is a well-understood science in business.[3] Using various techniques, business decisions can often be quantified down to a "go, no go" decision through various complex formulae, which are the substance of most MBA training programs. One only needs to look to the insurance industry to understand the depth that this level of decision-making can take on in complex organizations. Actuarial science, for example, is a "hard science" based upon probability and cohort survival techniques. Using powerful statistical techniques, most business decisions such as awarding favorable insurance rates to a group or an individual are data-driven to the greatest extent possible. Yet, statistical analysis aside, there is still the need for business acumen, political savvy, and expert judgment in these decisions. The same holds true for education. School districts experimenting with these technologies still must rely on their "informed intuition" and educational expertise before taking action on data findings. But those actions can become more informed through the systematic use and analysis of data.

The closest comparison that education has to this process is program evaluation. It is a premise of this book that practical, every-day program evaluation can be improved through enhancing "knowledge density"—improved understanding of the nature of the problem through greater access to relevant data. As the data we have to analyze become richer by virtue of the number of variables we can access over multiple years and across several cohorts, the database is considered to become more "dense." When we use decision support tools to explore that richly expanded database, our knowledge about the problems under review also becomes enriched. I term this richness and improvement in our understanding of the problem "knowledge density," a term borrowed from the information technology sector.[4] While the program evaluation literature in education is robust, it can be improved in everyday school practice through these procedures and technologies.

Where does this leave us as we enter the twenty-first century? As information technologies proliferate in the private sector and general government,

the demands placed on educational leaders to make better and quicker decisions will grow more intense. An increasing need will arise to develop "fast-
track evaluation methods" that use the essential elements of the best of our
program evaluation heritage. Through advances in information technologies,
many evaluation procedures that now take us months to gather and analyze
historical data will be completed in hours or even minutes. Educational leaders will need all of the skills that they now possess plus a new skill set: the ability to use and manipulate those technologies and techniques that I include
under the banner of "data-driven decision-making." Manny Fernandez, CEO
of the Gartner Group, looking ahead to the new century said it best: "Information technologies will be the crude oil of the twenty-first century." The
purpose of this book is to help advance the state of educational decision-
making. Data-driven decision-making techniques are defined and explained,
as is the role of emerging information technologies for school leadership.
Equally important will be a look at the new organizational structures and leadership necessary for successfully meeting the challenges of this new decade.
Hopefully it will help school leaders do a better job with school improvement.

Notes

1. Jeff Archer, "Under Amato, Hartford Schools Show Progress," *EdWeek* (March
2000), http://www.edweek.org/ew/ewstory.cfm?slug=25hartford.h19&keywords=Hartford.
2. Archer, "Under Amato."
3. Charles L. Smith Jr., *Computer-Supported Decision Making: Meeting the Decision Demands of Modern Organizations* (Greenwich, Conn.: Ablex Publishing Corporation, 1998).
4. Vasant Dhar and Roger Stein, *Seven Methods for Transforming Corporate Data into
Business Intelligence* (Upper Saddle River, N.J.: Prentice Hall, 1997).

CHAPTER ONE

~

What Is Data-Driven Decision-Making and Why Do It?

Data-driven decision-making is not anything new for most of business and industry as corporations have been practicing it for literally decades.[1–10] The most fundamental advantage that they have over education is their ability access to "corporate data" quickly and easily.[11–13] But we do not need to have an in-depth understanding of how corporate America works to recognize and appreciate the value of these technologies because they are all around us, impacting our everyday lives. In fact, in today's fast-paced world, it is hard to go through a day without encountering one or more of these technologies. For example, when we stop to fill up the car with gas we rarely use cash. To save time, we don't even have to go to the cash register. All we need to do is insert our credit/debit card, and our purchase is authorized over a computer network linked back to a data warehouse (a large repository of data). If we do not have enough money in our account, we will not be able to pump the gas. What is most fascinating about this technology is that we can be almost anywhere in the country and somehow that little machine on the gas pump knows whether we have enough money in our accounts back home to pay for the fill-up. While this may seem a novelty, it shouldn't, considering how long we have used credit cards. MasterCard, Visa, American Express, Diner's Club—these technologies are decades old and rely on that same technological base to "know" whether we have enough money in our accounts to pay for dinner, groceries, a new television, or a piece of jewelry.

However, the big difference today is the new, high-speed modem and transmission lines that enable access to these data warehouses in seconds. For

1

example, if we were to go into a drug store with a new prescription from our physician, the pharmacist could tell immediately if there might be a drug interaction with any other medications that we are taking. That's because he or she has access to a database showing our current medications and how the new medication might interact with any one or combination of them. When we go to the supermarket, electronic scanners make checkout lines faster and more accurate—another application of the same basic technology.

Sometimes these technologies are not so apparent. Each day, millions of passengers fly the nation's airlines. While in flight, special diagnostics ensure top performance of each jet engine. If the on-board system should indicate a deviation from the thousands of parameters programmed into the system (automated rule-based decision-making), special engine diagnostics determine the specific problem and identify a solution. This information is relayed to the destination airport and to a technician equipped with a CD-ROM reader detailing the specific problem and solution along with a list of parts that are needed—all in time for the plane to land to be serviced. In most of these cases, the problems are fixed in time for its next departure while the plane is sitting on the tarmac.

At the core of all of these innovations is a technology based on sophisticated relational databases that have grown up into data warehouses.[14] Literally, every time we make a purchase, pay a bill, make a phone call, or in some way communicate, we are using information technologies and some form of a data warehouse. Figure 1.1 demonstrates the disadvantage that school lead-

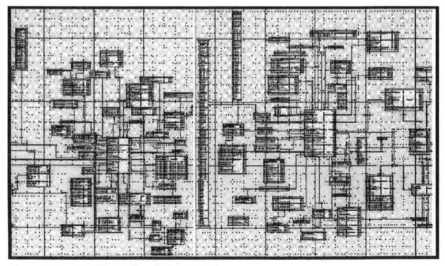

Figure 1.1   Multidimensional Data Warehouse

ers have over their private sector counterparts in making decisions quickly and more accurately. It shows a multidimensional data warehouse built for education (of typical complexity compared to one designed for the financial services sector) that allows users with these technologies to access all their "corporate" data on one computer screen, compared with a simple filing cabinet demonstrating how most educators must access information today.

The Need for Relational Databases

To deal with the complexity of our work, the first building block needed to efficiently conduct data-driven decision-making is to bring all of our educational data together for easy access and analysis. This requires a database that connects data from disparate data sources in a "relational" format. But creating one that is both dynamic and flexible to meet the changing needs and conditions in schools *and* one that is affordable is not easily accomplished.[15–18] While there are many examples where relational databases are used in schools for this purpose, they are typically found in large school systems that have management information staff and expertise. Some of the newer student operating systems designed ostensibly for student scheduling, attendance, grade reporting, and so on have some limited capacity for data warehousing. Although these systems can provide enhanced capability, they currently fall far short of the full operational ability needed to access and analyze *all* electronic data collected across the many disparate systems and platforms typically found in a school district. To achieve this goal school districts will need a data warehousing system specifically designed for this purpose.

Most schools, however, neither already have a management information system (MIS) department nor have they purchased one of the newer student operating systems with limited capacity for data analysis. Thus, data access and analysis remains a hands-on activity for most schools.[19]

The good news here is that data-driven decision-making can be conducted to some degree in the absence of advanced data warehousing applications using software tools such as common spreadsheet and database programs. Most of the examples in this book were conducted as hands-on projects.

Problem Solving and Problem Framing

Even when using advanced information technologies we know that 80 percent of problem solving is problem framing.[20] Consequently, the second building block of data-driven decision-making is the ability to effectively frame problems and develop a "concept map" that breaks the larger problem down into smaller, more manageable components for data analysis. Everyday problems encountered by school leaders are typically very complex in terms of the actual data analyses needed to properly address the issue. Questions such as "Is there any evidence of gender bias in our math program?" or "Can we identify performance targets based upon past cohort performance?" require that data from multiple sources be brought together for analysis. Our early research findings on the breadth and complexity of the questions educators must ask to effectively manage and lead their schools rivals that of the most complex questions and analyses conducted in the private sector.[21] Here are some examples taken from a pilot project in Connecticut looking at the use of information technologies in educational leadership:

1. What is the relationship between courses taken in grades six through ten and performance on the tenth-grade state mastery test in "integrated" learning? Also, what is the relationship between the eighth-grade state mastery holistic writing test and this tenth-grade integrated learning test?

2. Can the fourth-grade testing results be used to set performance targets for sixth grade?

3. What is the impact of instructional time on achievement at the elementary level?

4. How well do girls do in higher-level math courses compared to boys?

5. What is the relationship between eighth-grade holistic writing scores on the state mastery test and the response to literature scores on the tenth-grade mastery test for the same cohort? How can results in eighth grade be used to set improvement targets in tenth grade?

6. How many students took Algebra II as their highest math course and passed the tenth-grade mastery test in math? Geometry? Algebra I?

7. Which students are eligible for an alternative program based on the following criteria: two or more F grades in a semester; ten or more discipline referrals in the semester; ten or more absences in any course in the semester?

8. Do students who score below the goal on the integrated learning segment of the state mastery test take history in grade ten, specifically, World History II, an average level course? That is, does taking World History II contribute to success on the state mastery test, and should then a third year of history be mandated for all students?

9. For special education students, what is the relationship between their program and outcomes? What is the correlation between class grades

and standardized test scores? How often are special education students absent or suspended as compared to conventional students? What is the ability/achievement comparison of special education students? Are teachers grading fairly and properly? That is, what is the correlation between teachers' course grades to level of academic course difficulty?

10. What is the impact of student absenteeism on fourth-grade reading scores on the state mastery test?
11. How do student course-taking trends in mathematics in grades seven through ten impact achievement on high-stakes tests?

The problems of equity, student achievement, school improvement, and systemic reform seem daunting—but are solvable. They require access to historical data and an understanding of the key components of the problem. Moreover, problems such as these are too complex to answer in one step. They require multiple analyses covering the various subcomponents of the problem and then a consideration of the results of each sub-analysis in light of the whole—a process I refer to as a "helicopter view." Only then can a broad picture of the problem and potential solutions be understood.

Concept Maps

Two colleagues at the University of Connecticut (Barry Sheckley and Marijke Kerhahan) who work in the area of adult learning and problem solving have found that adults solve problems best when those problems are broken down into their key components or are "framed" in ways that make them more clear. They recommend the development of a "concept map" to identify the logical subcomponents of the problem that then become subanalyses. This process of breaking the problem down and conducting the analyses needed leads to a better understanding of the larger problem. Subsequent chapters follow this process of framing the problem more clearly, enabling more appropriate analyses and the consideration of results.

Data-Driven Decision-Making: Using Technology to Maximize Use of Our Time

Successful data-driven decision-making requires a six-step process. This process is outlined in Figure 1.2. It begins with identifying a problem and creating a concept map to frame the subcomponents of the problem, thereby developing a clear representation of the various subcomponents so that the data to be gathered and analyzed are fully understood. Step two requires that we actually gather the data and bring it into a single database or spreadsheet for analysis. (Although strategies and techniques for accomplishing this will be discussed in chapter 8, I do not want to minimize the challenge and difficulty in accomplishing this task. Even at very basic levels, this is highly complex and specialized work. It often represents the proverbial "brick wall" that educators hit when trying to conduct data-driven decision-making.) The third step in the process is to analyze the data for each of the subanalyses identified in the concept map representation of the problem. This too is a highly specialized process requiring an understanding of statistics and an ability to use statistical software. Once the various data analyses have been conducted, potential solutions can then be generated. The next step is to identify and implement best-fit solutions. The final step in the process is to monitor ongoing implementation and make adjustments as needed. Monitoring suggests evaluation, and it is through effective "fast-track" program evaluation that this ongoing monitoring and adjustment can be made.

As Figure 1.2 shows, most of our time, perhaps 90 percent or better, is spent on data gathering and analysis due to the complexity of these processes without the advantage of using information technologies. This leaves precious little time, 10 percent or so, available for solution generation and im-

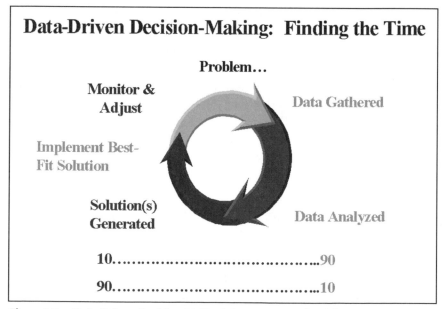

Figure 1.2   Data-Driven Decision-Making's Impact on Productivity

plementation. Use of new technologies just becoming available has the power to turn this time ratio around, freeing up valuable administrative time for those who perform the analyses to do what they do best: determine possible solutions and implement them.

Emerging New Technologies

There are several emerging school applications that use information technologies. Most schools are familiar with scheduling, grading, attendance, and other systems that are considered operational systems; that is, they perform some function in the running of the school. Data warehousing is also now emerging as an application that can draw data from many disparate systems without modifying or replacing those systems (see chapter 8). These applications are just now emerging and will likely become more common as the decade proceeds.[22-23] New initiatives are also under way to provide these applications totally on-line, eliminating the need for districts to buy and own expensive hardware and networking applications—an important consideration as technology improves dramatically every eighteen months or so. These services are provided as "application service providers" or ASPs. No doubt this is the wave of the near future as the costs to host and provide access to these technologies come down and as Internet bandwidth expands to improve data transmission speeds.

Using Data for Decision-Making and Improvement

The data used to conduct school improvement analyses can be grouped into three categories. Input variables (data) include student demographics, teacher background characteristics, budgetary resources, and any additional variables that we have little or no control over and consequently should be thought of as input variables. A second category includes the instructional processes such as the curriculum, teaching materials, professional development opportunities, and programs. The third category includes outcome measures, such as test results, class grades, dropout rates, graduation rates, and the post-secondary education enrollment rates of students. Together these three categories represent the universe of data elements that schools have access to and that need to be included in school improvement analyses. Figure 1.3 shows the relationship of these three categories of data. Most of the work conducted in schools is typically focused only on the third category. Only occasionally do we focus on student input variables as, for example, when we disaggregate data for equity analyses (by

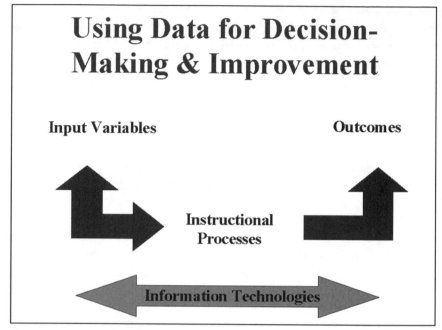

Figure 1.3   Categories of Data Variables

gender, race, ethnicity, SES, etc.). Certainly the need to conduct these queries for improving achievement is great.[24] But rarely do we focus our attention on the instructional processes employed in schools with any precision or regularity. Yet addressing critical school improvement problems requires analyses across *all three categories* of data (inputs, processes, and outcomes) to fully understand the range of possible solutions and interventions that have a chance to succeed. When the data become "more dense" through use of as many pertinent variables as possible, our fundamental understanding of the problem will become enriched, leading us to make better decisions.

Definition of Data-Driven Decision-Making

Data-driven decision-making can be defined as the process of selecting, gathering, and analyzing data to address school improvement or student achievement problems and challenges and acting on those findings. The critical components of what I refer to as fast-track evaluation and data-driven decision-making are understanding the problem and framing it into its logical component parts for analysis; gathering the needed data; conducting the appropriate analyses; generating possible solutions; and selecting a course of action to follow. Fast-track evaluation requires that we conduct an audit of existing (legacy) data (called a data audit) to determine if the problems under review can, in fact, be answered with the data readily available. If the data does not exist or is not readily accessible, then the question needs to be modified to fit that which can be answered within reasonable statistical limitations. Only as a last resort, when little or no useful data exists to address the basic questions under review, should we consider dropping the question altogether.

In many cases, school administrators have no choice but to respond immediately to the board or the public with the best information that they can quickly bring together. If issues continually arise for which there are no data but the questions are important to answer, it will be advantageous to develop a "data plan." That is, our task shifts to identifying what data are needed to address the question(s) and to make a determination if the cost/benefit of attaining those data is worthwhile. If the cost/benefit questions are answered satisfactorily, the plan should be implemented so that the needed data are available within two to three years.

The concept of conducting analyses based on limited available data should not be seen as a radical idea given what takes place in schools every day as educators are called upon to make decisions based on little or no data analysis and largely on "informed intuition."[25] These informed intuition decisions will be strengthened through the analyses of data but not replaced. The trick is to strike a balance between data analyses and the interpretation of those analyses based on years of wisdom and experience.

Using a fast-track evaluation process can improve the quality of administrative decision-making. Data-driven decision-making borrows practices from the program evaluation literature by (1) paying attention to which cohort groups are being analyzed and for what purposes, (2) determining what analyses should be conducted (making sure that these analyses are correct and appropriate to the questions under study), and (3) determining whether the available data is appropriate for the required analysis. Data-driven decision-making also uses the benchmarking process to measure progress toward the attainment of some desired goal or standard.

Data-driven decision-making and fast-track evaluation often (but not exclusively) use data warehouses, information technologies, and decision-support tools to access and analyze data quickly and easily. These processes rely on the use of "legacy data" (defined here as those data stored over time in a database for easy retrieval) to ensure that these data are available to make the analyses relevant. With data warehouses, the data can be refreshed weekly, monthly, or quarterly, providing relevant and recent data upon which to make decisions. But as we see in this book, there are many questions that can be addressed without these sophisticated technologies.

Inevitably, the decision as to what actions should be implemented as a result of data analyses requires judgment and experience. Data-driven decision-making is not a substitute for judgment, wisdom, and experience. Rather, it supports decision-makers in their decision-making processes. There is also a danger of placing too much importance on statistical analyses. Decisions should neither be totally "databased" nor should they be based solely on intuition. The desired mix should be decisions that are predicated on past practice experience and intuition—informed by data. And no decision should be made without consulting those most affected—the teachers. Using emerging information technology tools, one can envision a group of teachers and administrators sitting around a table, problem solving as they "drill down" into their data, gathering insights literally as fast as they can generate the questions.

Much Can Be Accomplished without These Technologies

There are many steps one can take without these advanced technologies using the basic principles and processes of data-driven decision-making. And you might be surprised to find that your district has some of these tools already built into the student information system. Regardless, there are many questions that can be asked and addressed by reviewing data reports and using basic analytical tools. Examples will be provided in this book that demonstrate what can be done and how much can actually be accomplished in a paper report environment.

Summary

This chapter has outlined the critical components of data-driven decision-making. Data-driven decision-making should be used for real problems that educators face every day as they manage and lead their schools toward improvement. As part of the program evaluation and benchmarking process, problems need to be mapped into their components so that they are fully understood, making clear the complexity of the required analyses and helping to generate potential solutions. I term the sum total of all of these processes and the sequence through which they are followed as an "integrated systems approach to school improvement" in which data-driven decision-making and fast-track program evaluation methods are used. Taken together, they constitute what we have come to term data-driven decision-making.

Notes

1. Charles L. Smith Jr., *Computer-Supported Decision Making: Meeting the Decision Demands of Modern Organizations* (Greenwich, Conn.: Ablex Publishing Corporation, 1998).

2. Vasant Dhar and Roger Stein, *Seven Methods for Transforming Corporate Data into Business Intelligence* (Upper Saddle River, N.J.: Prentice Hall, 1997).

3. Max H. Bazerman, *Judgment in Managerial Decision Making* (New York: John Wiley & Sons, 1990).

4. Mairead Browne, *Organizational Decision Making and Information* (Norwood, N.J.: Ablex Publishing Corporation, 1993).

5. William L. Carlson, *Cases in Managerial Data Analysis* (Boston, Mass.: Duxbury Press, 1997).

6. Jerwin Jou, James Shanteau, and Richard Jackson Harris. "An Information Processing View of Framing Effects: The Role of Casual Schemas in Decision Making," *Memory & Cognition* 24 (Jan. 1996): pp. 1–15.

7. Ralph L. Keeney, *Value Focused Thinking: A Path to Creative Decision Making* (Cambridge, Mass.: Harvard University Press, 1992).

8. David J. McLaughlin, "Strengthening Executive Decision Making," *Human Resource Management* 34 (Fall 1995): pp. 443–461.

9. Frank M. Messina and Sanjay Singh, "Executive Information Systems: Not Just for Executives Anymore!" *Management Accounting* 77 (July 1995): pp. 60–63.

10. Alan J. Rowe and Sue Anne Davis, *Intelligent Information Systems: Meeting the Challenge of the Information Era* (Westport, Conn.: Greenwood Publishing Group, 1996).

11. Ben-Zion Barta, Moshe Telem, and Yaffa Gev, *Information Technology in Educational Management* (New York: Chapman & Hall, 1994).

12. P. Streifer, "Database Decision-Making through Fast-Track Evaluation: What Is It and Why Do It?" *Invited publication—Schools in the Middle Journal* (a publication of the National Association of Secondary School Principals) (September 1999).

13. P. Streifer, "Putting the 'Byte' in Educational Decision-Making," Commentary, *Ed Week* (March 1999).

14. W. H. Inmon, *Building the Data Warehouse,* second edition (New York: John Wiley & Sons, 1996).

15. Melissa A. Cook, *Building Enterprise Information Architectures: Reengineering Information Systems* (Upper Saddle River, N.J.: Prentice Hall, 1996).

16. Alan R. Simon, *Data Warehousing for Dummies* (Foster City, Calif.: IDG Books Worldwide, 1997).

17. Jae K. Skim, Joel Siegel, and Robert Chi, *The Vest-Pocket Guide to Information Technology* (Paramus, N.J.: Prentice Hall, 1997).

18. Richard Saul Wurman, *Information Architects* (New York: Watson-Guptill Publications, 1997).

19. L. Kangshem, "Smart Data: Mining the School District Data Warehouse," *Electronic School* (September 1999).

20. Barry G. Sheckley and Morris T. Keeton, *Improving Employee Development: Perspectives from Research and Practice* (Chicago: Council for Adult and Experiential Learning, 1997).

21. P. Streifer and M. Shibles, "What are the Important Questions? Database School Improvement through Comprehensive Information Management: The CT Academy/KPMG/UConn Partnership" (paper presented at the American Educational Research Association, Montreal, Canada, April 1999).

22. Kangshem, "Smart Data."

23. "Software for Data Use," *The School Administrator* 58, no. 4 (April 2001).

24. Ruth S. Johnson, *Setting Our Sights: Measuring Equity in School Change* (Los Angeles, Calif.: Achievement Council, 1996).

25. Jerry Hirshberg, *The Creative Priority: Driving Innovative Business in the Real World* (New York: Harper Business, 1998).

CHAPTER TWO

Longitudinal Analyses for Program Evaluation, Benchmarking, and Setting Improvement Targets

This chapter addresses one of the most important areas or frames of data-driven decision-making—reviewing trends in performance, over time and among multiple cohorts, to provide better insights into the problem at hand and to develop more successful interventions. Why look at performance trends over time and across multiple cohorts? Because doing so gives us a sense of perspective as all of our analyses, no matter how sophisticated statistically, will always remain somewhat unreliable (for decision-making) due to the very nature of the variables we measure.

We all recognize that there are very few, if any, absolutes in education; there will always be gray areas—no clear-cut definitive solutions to complex problems. For example, the most reliable measures (statistically speaking) we have to assess student performance and thus to analyze are standardized test items. But these tests (and their test items) are often criticized for addressing too narrow a band of student learning, the very consequence of making them valid and reliable. The everyday observations we make also tend to be weak unless the observers have had extensive reliability training in rigorous qualitative evaluation techniques—an unrealistic expectation in everyday school life. Student portfolios, too, are subject to numerous "threats to reliability and validity" (the technical phrase to describe the problem) while "performance tests" are often subject to substantial measurement bias, problems that can be solved with training for assessors but take more time and resources than is typically available for school districts.

So where does all of this uncertainty leave us? The answer, if there is one, is to look at trends of student achievement over time and across multiple cohorts as the key indicators of achievement. Like correlational research in which causality cannot be known, program evaluation, or fast-track evaluation, is subject to similar limitations because we are looking at relationships between and among imprecise variables that are used to measure performance in less than perfect research designs. But like correlational research where insights are gained over time and multiple analyses, where a preponderance of the evidence indicates that a relationship exists, fast-track evaluation and decision-making can be strengthened through an examination of performance trends of multiple cohorts over time. Thus the most productive analysis strategy we can use in data-driven decision-making (and fast-track evaluation) is longitudinal analysis that uses the basic techniques of trend analysis.

In summary then, trend analyses conducted over time therefore constitute longitudinal analyses. And conducting longitudinal analyses will increase our confidence that we are addressing a real problem, not just a one-time anomaly.

Knowledge Density

Conducting analyses of multiple cohorts over time yields maximum knowledge density (a concept that is fully explored in chapter 8). Knowledge density, a term borrowed from the information technology sector,[1] occurs as the data we have to analyze become richer as the number of variables that we use increases over multiple years of data across increasing cohorts of students. Realistically though, performing iterative analyses over multiple cohorts can only be done in an information technology (IT) data warehousing environment. In the absence of this high-tech environment, we can still do data-driven decision-making, but we will be limited in our ability to perform *multiple trend analyses* due to realistic time and resource constraints. In such settings knowledge density can improve, but just marginally. Should we then rely on these limited paper and pencil processes to make decisions? Yes, because there are many examples where schools have made substantial progress at improving achievement through these approaches. It comes down to the fact that some information properly interpreted is inevitably better than none.

Major Purposes of Longitudinal Evaluation

There are two major purposes for conducting longitudinal analyses. First, longitudinal analyses should be conducted to determine reasons that might explain current performance levels so that instructional changes can be made. Longitudinal analyses should be conducted to help predict future performance by setting targets for future performance through benchmarking. To accomplish the first purpose, that is, to determine reasons that might explain current performance, we might review a group's past performance to see if there were any early indications of problems. We would also want to compare this group's performance to that of previous and similar groups to help us understand why current performance is not what was expected.

If we wanted to establish performance targets for a particular cohort of students, the second purpose, we would need to understand the students' previous achievement levels on various performance measures in comparison to similar groups so that reasonable but challenging targets could be established. Here we are using past performance to predict future performance. Examples follow that demonstrate both of these major purposes.

Reviewing Past Performance to Determine Reasons That Might Explain Current Performance to Guide Instructional Changes

Data-driven decision-making's greatest strength lies in its ability to drive instructional change based on a review of past performance. Examples in this chapter range from the selection of reading materials in the elementary school to determining why Scholastic Achievement Test (SAT) performance improved or declined. The following examples will demonstrate the power of these techniques for school improvement.

A Real-Life Example

I was superintendent of the Avon, Connecticut, public schools in the mid-1990s and identified a major student performance problem in the district. Our schools, as part of a strategic planning process, undertook an analysis of overall performance on the state mastery (administered in grades four, six, eight, and ten) test to find ways in which improvements could be made. The board and I had been concerned over the district's lack of improvement for the past several years, especially in light of the apparent improvement by comparative school districts over that same time period. To clearly understand the big picture, the curriculum director created the graph in Figure 2.1.

The graph shows the total percent of Avon students who reached mastery on the state mastery test over a three-year period compared to the same information for six similar districts. The data are displayed as a simple line

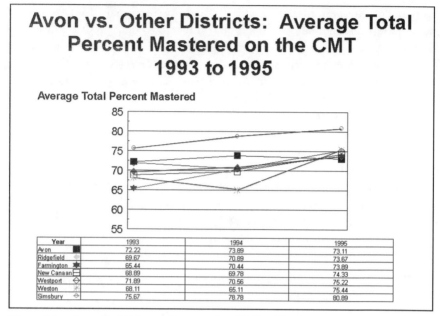

Avon vs. Other Districts: Average Total Percent Mastered on the CMT 1993 to 1995

Average Total Percent Mastered

Year		1993	1994	1995
Avon	■	72.22	73.89	73.11
Ridgefield	◇	69.67	70.89	73.67
Farmington	★	65.44	70.44	73.89
New Canaan	⊟	68.89	69.78	74.33
Westport	⊖	71.89	70.56	75.22
Weston	✳	68.11	65.11	75.44
Simsbury	⊖	75.67	78.78	80.89

Figure 2.1   Avon Performance Compared to Similar Districts

graph along with the actual data in the table below (this graph was created in Freelance Graphics and can be easily created in programs such as Power-Point, Excel, or any other basic graphing program). Providing the actual data (percentages) in a table below the graph is useful because it allows further inspection of the data without cluttering the graph. All of these data were readily available on reports from the Connecticut Department of Education, making data extraction or collection easy.

We can see that Avon's performance was relatively static over the three-year period. At the same time, most of the other districts started at or below Avon's performance level and then equaled or slightly bettered their performance. Simsbury's performance started out higher than Avon's and then improved even further to exceed it substantially.

Emerging Questions

Two questions emerged from this basic review. First, what was Simsbury doing to propel it ahead of all of these districts and, second, what had all the other districts done to now equal Avon's performance? Another way of looking at the problem was: Why was Avon's performance static while all other districts were making improvement? Joel Barker, who coined the phrase "paradigm shift," has also said that "One's past performance or reputation is absolutely no guarantee of future success."[2] Avon had been proud of its high level of student achievement, but it now looked as though we were losing ground to other districts. Put another way, the board was concerned that students in competitive districts were outperforming students at Avon, putting them at an educational disadvantage. On a deeper level, the Avon administrative team became concerned that the instructional techniques and materials used in similar districts were more powerful than those they were using. That being the case, Avon students could be at a significant educational disadvantage, all the other political issues aside, if the situation was not understood and corrected. The concept map outlining this problem is shown in Figure 2.2.

The initial review led to a series of logical questions. What was Avon doing differently, if anything, from these comparative districts? Were Avon's instructional materials aligned to the curriculum and were they of sufficient rigor? Although the district had purchased a new reading series only three years prior, many teachers were complaining that the materials were too easy for many of their students, indicating that they had to supplement with additional readings.

These discussions led to a follow-up analysis looking at whether the instructional materials used in Avon were of sufficient rigor (against external standards). The director of curriculum, who initially raised this issue, tested all of Avon's materials for reading difficulty (DRP level) against two standards: other texts available and the state reading mastery goal in grades four, six, eight, and ten.

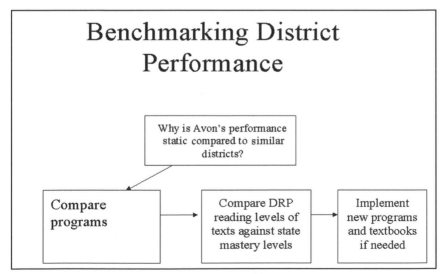

Figure 2.2   Concept Map of District Performance Problem

First he looked at the DRP level of Avon's existing reading instruction materials as compared to other reading series that were commercially available at the time. As shown in Figure 2.3, the materials in use by Avon had an average DRP rating five points below that of other available texts by fifth grade. It was also lower at the critical entry level of kindergarten. The graph also notes that the average DRP level of these materials drops off at fifth grade, thereafter crossing the lower threshold of the state mastery goal.

Alarmed by this finding the director of curriculum decided to conduct similar analyses for all the other instructional materials in use by the district through tenth grade—to the extent data were available. Figure 2.4 shows the summary data for English/language texts in use. We can see that the texts in use by the English and language arts department in grades K–5 were a full ten DRP points below others commercially available and that the DRP of the language arts materials also crossed the lower threshold of the state mastery goal in grade five. Figure 2.5 shows the same findings for the social studies texts in use throughout the district. Finally, the curriculum director looked at the target grade level equivalent of Avon's reading materials for third grade as compared to other available materials and found, as shown in Figure 2.6,

DRP Level of Avon Reading Materials vs. State Goal and Others Available

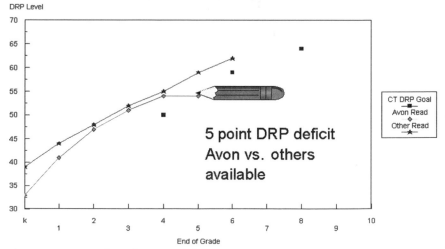

Figure 2.3   DRP of Reading Materials

DRP Level of Avon English Language Books vs. State Goal and Others Available

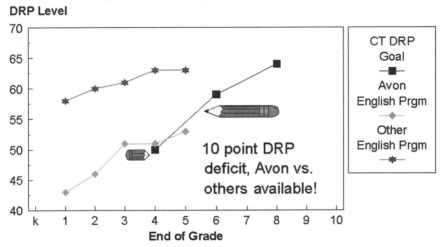

Figure 2.4   DRP of English Materials

DRP Level of Avon Social Studies Materials vs. State Goal

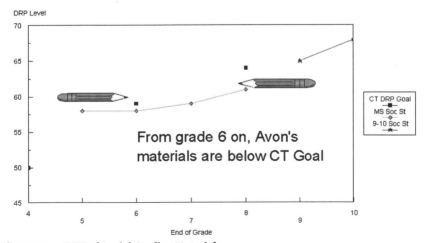

Figure 2.5   DRP of Social Studies Materials

Grade Level Equivalents: Avon Reading vs. Others Available

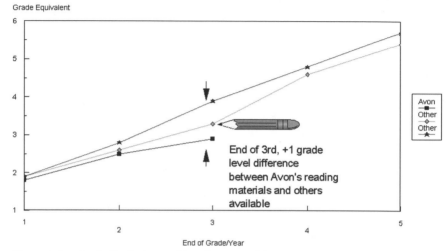

Figure 2.6   Grade Equivalents of Reading Materials

that there was a full one-year reading level deficit by the time students reached this point in their program.

To gather all of this data, the curriculum director used various references to chart the DRP level of the instructional materials, looking up specific publisher statements reporting DRP level, or he tested the materials himself with a commercially available DRP assessment program. He then simply placed his findings in a graphing program.

Actions Taken

It has been said that a picture is worth a thousand words, and it certainly applied in this case. Armed with this overwhelming evidence, I used these very graphs in a presentation to the board of education to seek budget funds for a complete overhaul of the reading program. I also laid out a plan to replace all the other texts over the next three years. The board reacted in common unity but uncommon speed authorizing the expenditures and placing them at the highest priority level for the upcoming budget. Not willing to wait the six months to the beginning of the next budget cycle, the board authorized an initial expenditure to begin staff and curriculum development immediately (in February) in preparation for the summer and new budget cycle that was to begin on July 1.

This case study demonstrates the power of inquiry, analysis, and decision-making followed by thoughtful actions designed to improve the quality of students' educational experience. While we could argue that this initiative began as a concern for test score performance and competition among school districts, in reality it turned out to be an issue of much deeper concern and importance. As we have seen here, test scores can be an indicator of a more deeply rooted instructional problem. Had the follow-up analyses shown no real difference in program rigor, then driving test scores higher for the simple sake of political expediency would have been a waste of time or worse, as such myopic focus can be dysfunctional for the organization. But when used to uncover real instructional problems, standardized tests accompanied by sound analyses and intervention can be powerful tools for change.

A Complex School Improvement Problem and the Value of a Data Warehouse

For a more in-depth example of how to identify reasons that might explain current performance levels (to drive instructional changes), consider the following true case. Literally every school district in the nation today is concerned with student achievement. Whether driven by state mastery tests or nationally standardized tests, the pressures for accountability and improved student achievement grow daily. District and school performance on these tests also affect budgets in many communities, adding to the pressure of accountability and the need to find the causes of poor achievement to design solutions.

Recently a district in the northeast experienced a significant drop in their student SAT scores. This suburban school district had enjoyed high and stable SAT scores for a number of years and all of a sudden experienced a twenty-three-point drop in verbal achievement and a twenty-five-point drop in math achievement for an overall decline of forty-eight points on the SAT test. This obviously led to the broad question: "Why did our SAT scores go down?" Because of the interrelationship between SAT performance and numerous school and student variables, the analysis of this problem and the identification of potential solutions posed a real challenge because it is a highly complex activity and not easily achieved. In reality, this particular school district spent five months gathering and analyzing the data before it could begin to implement solutions. The concept map in Figure 2.7 represents the logical components of the problem that were then turned into data analyses (and that could also be thought of as separate research questions all relating to the larger problem under study).

Logical Analysis and Inquiry

The concept map identifies the lines of inquiry needed to address the larger question or problem under study. In this example, a subset question would be whether this particular cohort, the class of 1998, had previously experienced poor test results that might have been picked up and dealt with earlier. If that was not the case, then given the past experience of the district, having achieved steady and high SAT performance for many years, one could conclude that the problem was central to the high school as opposed to earlier grade levels. Consequently, one logical analysis would be to look at other tests that had been administered to this particular cohort, such as the PSAT, and the tenth, eighth, and sixth grade mastery tests that are administered in this particular state.

We also know that one of the best predictors of SAT performance is course rigor, which leads to questions revolving around those courses taken by this class. What courses were taken? How rigorous were they? And how well did students perform in them? This line of questioning is also represented in Figure 2.7 as a separate analysis from the question of whether this cohort had performed

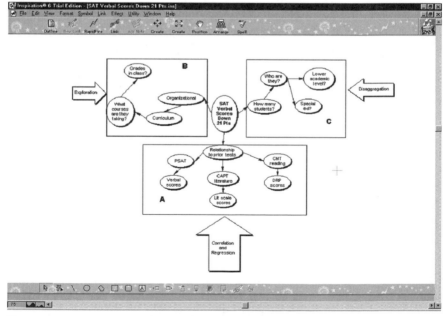

Figure 2.7   Concept Map of SAT Achievement Problem

poorly on previous tests and the implications of such a finding. A third subset of questions arise concerning student demographics: How long were students enrolled in this particular high school; what do we know about their attendance rates; and how many hours do students work at part-time jobs? All of these factors could affect SAT performance, making them candidates for review.

Actions Taken

The actual results of the analyses in this district yielded two major findings. First, the courses taken by this cohort were not as rigorous as previous groups, and second, certain bands of students (between the 50th and 70th local percentiles) were not performing as well as students in previous cohorts. The resulting actions were: (1) to discuss course-taking trends with the middle school and high school guidance counselors (and teachers), hopefully to steer students toward more rigorous courses and to improve follow-up between the school and home to aid parents in helping their children perform better in class, and (2) to implement improved programs for students between the 50th and 70th local percentiles to bolster their verbal and quantitative skills.

Trends over Time and Use of the Data Cube for Representing the Analysis

In their private-sector work on decision-making, Inmon[3] and Dhar and Stein[4] show us another way of looking at complex problems in the representation of a data cube. The data cube is best used to represent problems and data collection over time, through multiple dimensions or variables. Through our preliminary work in Connecticut we have found the data cube representation is particularly useful as a next-step beyond the concept map to further break down and compartmentalize the subcomponents of each of the analyses identified in the concept map. Figure 2.8 presents a graphic representation of the previously discussed SAT problem in a data cube format.

Adding the Dimension of Time

As noted above, in addition to providing a clear representation of the problem, the added dimension in the data cube representation is that of time. For example, one analysis would be the relationship between this cohort's SAT scores with their PSATs in eleventh grade, then their tenth and eighth grade scores as a longitudinal trend analysis. After that the district would want to analyze which courses students took over their high school career (looking at rigor) and also the sequence of those courses. Logically they would also want to look at what grades students received in each of those courses and in various course

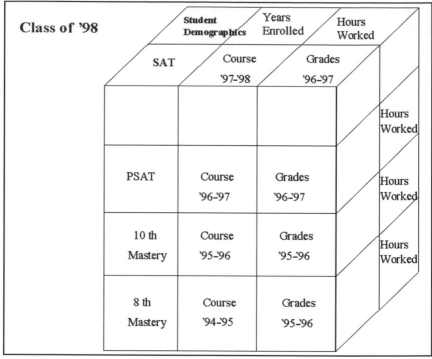

Figure 2.8   Data Cube of SAT Achievement Problem

sequences. These analyses would be followed up by looking at the demographic issues discussed earlier of when students enrolled, how long they work, absentee rates, and so on, assuming that the data were easily available.

Deeper and More Complex Analyses

As problems become more and more complex, requiring analyses across multiple years/cohorts, the data cube representation helps us understand and frame the various subsets of required analyses. For example, if we wanted a deeper understanding of what happened with this specific cohort of students (class of 1998), we would logically need to compare all of these analyses with that of previous cohorts. So, if we conducted the initial analysis with the class of 1998, we would want to repeat these analyses for the classes of 1997 and 1996 and compare the results across all three cohorts to understand the trends at work and to implement the best-fit solutions. Figure 2.9 presents the three-dimensional nature of this larger question.

Problems as complex as this one require decision support tools that go beyond basic tools such as spreadsheet programs and the limited data analysis currently provided by some student information systems. Complex problems like these in

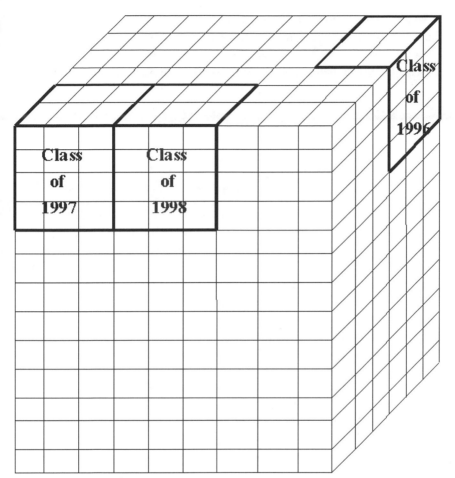

Figure 2.9 Data Cube Expanded

the private sector led to the development of data warehousing, information technologies, and sophisticated decision-support tools. Solving complex problems of this nature using decision-support tools will be the subject of chapter 8.

In the SAT case described here, district personnel took almost five months to gather and analyze what data they could to identify problems and engineer interventions. But they were limited to one cohort dimension, that is, looking at the class of 1998. Their conclusions about cohort performance and course-taking rigor were not fully explored due to the sheer volume of data that needed to be collected (over three cohorts). As is the case in most school and school districts, these data were not readily accessible. Hence, district personnel reviewed what data they could easily acquire and then used their "informed intuition" to extrapolate findings.

More thorough analyses across multiple years and cohorts as shown in Figure 2.9 would realistically require the use of a data warehouse. Queries that can be built in minutes with data warehouses allow for the easy and quick gathering and analysis of data across multiple years and cohorts to hone in on problems in ways that are only possible through multiple-dimension trend analyses. Thus, these emerging technologies can be immensely useful for drilling down to conduct longitudinal data analyses over multiple cohorts and years.

Reviewing Past Performance to Establish Performance Targets

Another major purpose of conducting longitudinal analyses is to set performance targets for a certain group of students (cohort), grade level, school, or even school district. In the following example we will focus on a specific grade level, and our goal will be to set performance targets in reading for the current eighth-grade cohort as tenth graders (two years down the road) based on analyses of data from previous groups of students.

Establish a Baseline

A goal for schools should be to improve student performance over time and across several groups of students, especially across organizational units (grades six to eight and nine to twelve). If, for example, historical reading achievement levels remained relatively stable from eighth to tenth grade, and if the average student was performing at around the 60th national percentile, then the goal should be to raise performance to the 70th or 75th percentile. (Note: We could say the same for elementary to middle school or from early elementary to later elementary levels. The question could also be modified for other variables such as to identify what level of student dropout rate should be aimed for over the next three years. In this example we will stay with the middle/high school configuration and focus on reading achievement levels.) The main idea here is to develop a baseline performance level and then to use that baseline to set a reasonable target over the ensuing three-year period. The summary data for this analysis is represented in Table 2.1.

Table 2.1 Average National Percentile Ranking of Student Reading Performance

	8th Grade Performance	10th Grade Performance
Group A	60th	63rd
Group B	58th	60th
Current Group	60th	x

Benchmarking to External and Internal Standards

Here we see that the reading performance of two previous cohorts, groups A and B, was generally stable from eighth to tenth grade; that is, there was little improvement. Group A's performance improved only slightly from the 60th to the 63rd national percentile. Group B's improvement was no better. The current eighth-grade group, the group for whom we want to establish an improvement target, is performing at the same level as the other two groups when they were in eighth grade. Therefore, one could argue that a reasonable target might be the 70th percentile. But is that reasonable? Is it too low? To find out we could look at two additional sets of data. First, if possible, we would *benchmark* our students' performance to that of similar districts using the same performance measures. (Your state might produce a district report card of state mastery tests in which these data are included. For example, the State Department of Education in Connecticut produces a searchable Web site with volumes of district and school performance data that can be used to make these comparisons [www.state.ct.us/sde/ssp.htm]. Many states include such information for public access over the World Wide Web on their state education department's Web site. As in Connecticut, many states now also provide these comparative data across school districts and schools. As a last resource it would be useful to call the school or district that you believe is a good comparison to share aggregate data results.) If in using these resources we find that the external benchmark or comparison group's performance was in the same range in tenth grade as our previous comparative groups (60th to 65th percentile), then a performance target for the current group set at the 70th percentile would be reasonable.

Drill Back Further in Time for Deeper Understanding

But to gain a better understanding of what might be possible, we might also want to review additional cohorts' reading performance data and "drill" or look further back in time to these groups' sixth-grade performance levels. So far we have only reviewed two cohorts, groups A and B, over two testing periods (eighth and tenth grades). But are there other cohorts that might have done better and, if so, what were their characteristics? What about six-year trends instead of three? If these data yield more information (knowledge density) we could use this new information to set a more challenging target (if the data warranted doing so). These data are shown in Table 2.2.

In this case the additional data review has yielded important new information. First, we can see that group C started out at the same place as group

Table 2.2   Expanded Analysis—Drilling Back in Time

	6th Grade Performance	8th Grade Performance	10th Grade Performance
Group A (1999)	50th	60th	63rd
Group B (1998)	55th	58th	60th
Group C (1997)	55th	65th	70th
Current Group (2000)	60th	60th	x

B in sixth grade, but they excelled over that group in eighth and also tenth grade. Therefore, it is reasonable to assume that further levels of growth are possible. Group C is a full three years older than the current group; therefore we would want to ask a clarifying question: What was different about this group or the school that might explain its higher performance? Moreover, by looking back to sixth grade, we can now see that the group for whom we are establishing a benchmark, the current group, had higher levels of achievement than all the other groups except that its achievement "flattened" out in eighth grade. This leads us to ask whether something might be going on in the middle grades to depress achievement. In summary, after looking at *all* if these issues, it should be possible to set a higher performance target for our current group to the 75th national percentile.

The Drill-Down Process: Logical Exploration Achieving a Mix of Quantitative and Qualitative Analyses

It is important to recognize that this basic data review only leads us to ask broader, deeper questions about the schooling experience. This process of logical exploration back in time is referred to as the drill-down process. Looking beyond the hard, quantitative data, review of qualitative issues adds meaning and provides direction for our actions. Conducting quantitative data analyses without asking such follow-up questions is a serious mistake and will likely lead to misdirected actions. Conversely, asking qualitative questions without first using available data to set a direction will often result in too much process and a possible waste of valuable time and resources. The ideal mix is to use quantitative data analysis to lead one to the deeper qualitative questions as in this example. Thus, we should think of longitudinal data analysis as a compass that helps points us in a particular direction. But we need wisdom and experience to help navigate and understand what lies before us.

Any school should be able to perform these analyses using simple descriptive statistics, especially the example discussed looking at prior performance over three years and two groups. The data collection becomes just a little more complex for the second example looking back to sixth grade and adding another group.

Data Extraction or Collection

Data extraction for these analyses was straightforward—we simply copied aggregate student performance data that was available from a general report of the testing agencies (or state) and placed that data into a chart for our use. And in each of these cases we have only looked at one dependent variable, or measure, for each group: average national percentile rank of reading performance on a standardized test. Life gets a lot more complicated when we want to sort the groups based on specific learning objectives within a subject area such as measurement or computation within the math program or grammar, language usage, or writing within the language arts program. Moreover, if we wanted to do more than look at descriptive statistics and correlate performance across groups, the details, or specific student data would have to be in a database—not limited to aggregate data as used here. In cases where we want to drill down into the data source and "mine" it for possibly hidden findings, IT and data warehousing are needed (see chapter 8).

Concept Maps and Data Cubes: Representing More Complex and Deeper Problems

The concept map for the first analysis—looking at two groups over three years to form a baseline reading performance level, is shown in Figure 2.10. Here we are using tenth-grade standardized test data (expressed as average national percentiles) from cohorts A and B to set a target for a new group of students about to enter high school. Thus, we are gaining an understanding of student performance levels by reviewing how well previous students have performed in an effort to set a reasonable improvement target for the new group of students.

We then looked further back in time to improve our understanding of prior student achievement levels to help set this performance target. Figure 2.11 is a data cube representation of this problem in which we are looking back in time to when cohorts A, B, and C were sixth graders.

Adding Variables and Complexity

Since this analysis revealed new, important information about achievement levels for these groups, it might now be worthwhile to bring another variable

Longitudinal Evaluation for
Setting Improvement Targets

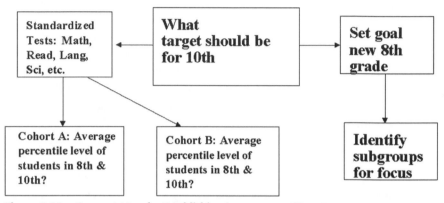

Figure 2.10   Concept Map for Establishing Improvement Targets

into consideration—student ability. The essential question now becomes whether school programs are attaining maximum achievement based on average student or cohort ability. (A cautionary note is needed here about using student ability scores from tests such as the Metropolitan, Stanford, and California achievement tests. Many would argue that these tests are very limited in what they measure, and in any event, one must be careful to use these ability scores only when curriculum and test objectives match. These concerns are very important and should be heeded. In our case study, we are matching the specific test to the school objectives under review—all tied to an ability score provided on the achievement test. So, with this alignment, we should be able to glean further meaning from this analysis as it affects the focused goal of setting an improvement target for the new group.)

Figure 2.11 shows student reading achievement reported as national percentiles, as already discussed in this example. However, this new analysis will require more sophisticated techniques than simply looking at average national percentiles over time. Rather, a powerful statistical technique called *analysis of covariance* will be needed to factor in student ability. Analysis of covariance is a complex statistical analysis that requires someone with a background in statistics to run and interpret the results. The important point here is that such analyses are possible and could yield even more important

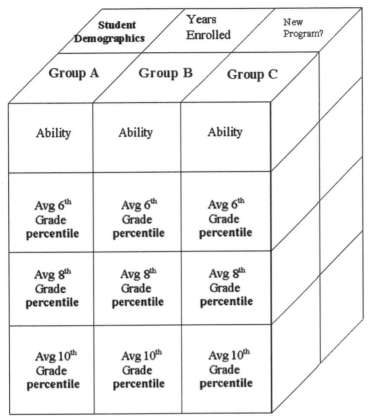

Figure 2.11   Data Cube: Reading Achievement, Verbal Ability, and Other Variables

and detailed findings than before. In this case it did, showing that group C had the ability to perform at even higher levels (making a performance target of the 75th national percentile doable).

Back to the Real World—State Mastery Results

Many state mastery tests now report aggregate results expressed as the number or percent of students reaching state goal, rather than percentiles as used earlier. Student scores are then reported as the percent meeting goal and perhaps some range such as proficient versus needing improvement that could indicate some level of performance at or below goal attainment. In such cases the discussion throughout this section applies simply by replacing "percent of students attaining goal" for "average national percentile." The important point is to recognize what metric is being used and how it needs to be interpreted.

For example, "average performance at the 60th national percentile" and "60 percent of students" at some level of achievement have entirely different meanings and interpretations. In the first case, we interpret the statistic as our "average" student performed better than 60 percent of the student who took this test. The classic definition of a percentile point, in this case "the 60th percentile," is the value above which 40 percent of the observed cases fall and below which 60 percent of the observed cases fall. But this tells us nothing about how well our students did against a performance standard; it only tells us how well our students did as compared to all observed cases. What happens if all students did poorly or did really well? Thus, this statistic can be misleading if the standard is not understood or is too low or too high for our population and curriculum.

We interpret the second statistic (the percent of students who attain a goal point) as a true local readout of performance against some well established standard. The classic definition here is the percentage of local cases having a particular value. Thus, the "particular value" is defined—in this case the state mastery standard—and we have a true readout on local student achievement levels.

Both measures or metrics are useful—they are just different. And its important to keep their meanings and interpretations clear so that proper conclusions can be drawn.

Hartford Case Study—Simplifying
the Representation of Data

The Hartford, Connecticut, public schools were in serious need of improvement on all levels and in every subject area. After numerous changes in the superintendency and a state take over, nothing seemed to be working. The new superintendent, Anthony Amato, came on board in May 1999 with a now locally famous pledge, "Hartford will never again be last" (in state mastery test scores). To drive improvement throughout the district, a number of systemic changes have been implemented with the improvement process driven by a data-driven decision-making strategy.

The key question facing the district was where to begin. The state provided a wealth of data in the form of reports, charts, and graphs, but it all could be a confusing mess to those unfamiliar with interpreting statistics and charts—having to pour over reams of data. This problem is not unlike the difficulties many of us have in reading corporate financial reports—as we find ourselves asking which data are important. What should I pay attention to? The problem of data presentation for effective decision-making has been addressed by Tufte[5,6] and reviewed here in chapter 7. From Tufte's work we know that providing decision-makers piles and piles of reports can often make the problem of analysis and decision-making more difficult, or worse, can result in erroneous conclusions. To solve this problem, Hartford asked The CT Academy for Education, Connecticut's statewide systemic initiative organization (under the National Science Foundation), to see if it could help in the presentation of mathematics achievement data. The CT Academy contracted a software company to write a computer program that extracted the necessary data from Hartford's mastery test database provided by the state and transform that data into a straightforward set of graphs that teachers, principals, parents, and central office administrators could use to more clearly understand achievement and to plan interventions. Many authors have extolled the virtues of simplistic data representation for driving improvements, such as Bernhardt[7] and Johnson.[8] Figure 2.12 is an example from one of the Hartford Schools.

South Middle School had made better progress on the state mastery test than the Hartford average over the prior six years as noted in Figure 2.12.

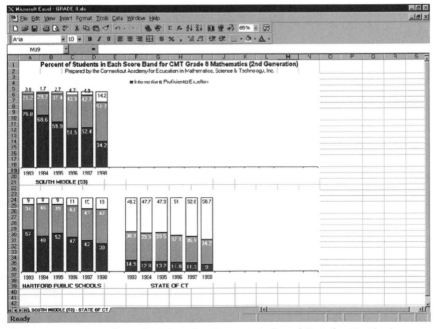

Figure 2.12   CT Academy for Education Representation of Data for Hartford

The percent of students in the lowest performance level, "intervention," declined from 75.8 percent in 1993 to 34.2 percent in 1998. In this case mathematics achievement levels improved at this school to a greater extent than the district as a whole. During this same time period, the Hartford public schools as a whole showed some, but not as dramatic, improvement in this performance band with the percent of students in the intervention band going from 57 to 38 percent. Each Hartford school was provided similar reports to gauge its overall performance.

Additional improvements, however, would require more specific data. Therefore, The CT Academy also developed these graphs for each learning objective (in mathematics). This particular mathematics test is comprised of forty objectives. An example set of performance data is shown in Figure 2.13 for South Middle School.

While learning improved on most mathematics objectives over the six-year period at levels similar to objectives 29 and 30 at South Middle School, there were areas that experienced outstanding growth such as objectives 28 and 32. It would be important for South Middle School to understand those factors that contributed to this significant improvement. As an improvement

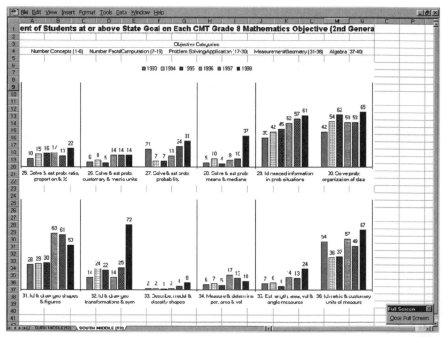

Figure 2.13   CT Academy for Education Representation of Data for South Middle School, Hartford

strategy, it is doubtful that further quantitative analysis of this objective (using the state mastery test data) will yield important information; instead, the school improvement team should interview staff, students, and parents to determine what they believe contributed to students' improvement in "Solving and Estimating Problems—Means and Medians" and "Identification and Drawing Geometric Transformations and Symbols." Were new materials and teaching techniques introduced? Did teachers focus on these specific learning objectives/areas? If that was the case, their emphasis was successful while not impacting all the other mathematics learning objectives.

These graphs have also identified specific learning areas in which little or no growth occurred, such as objectives 25, 26, 27, 33, 34, and 35. Depending on what interventions worked for objectives 28 and 32, hopefully those same general techniques can now be applied to learning in these objectives/areas.

By compiling complex data into an easy-to-read format, faculty and administration are able to quickly identify areas in need of improvement and areas of success. Armed with this information, staff are able to talk through these issues in search of new ways to improve instruction. This was the case in one Hartford school where a student of mine took these mathematics achievement data and drilled down with her principal and school improvement team to find specific areas of focus for improvement. In doing so she identified a number of areas in need of further study. For example, after eliminating obvious variables like previous learning levels of the students and staff turnover, she began looking at the mathematics materials and texts in use over the previous five years (not unlike the Avon case study discussed earlier). She found that one particular mathematics text had been in use for only eighteen months, but during that time period achievement appeared to rise more significantly than in other years (several texts were in use for short periods of time over the previous five-year period). She could not ascertain why the district had implemented so many math series in such a short time frame, but she did isolate an important variable through her drilling-down process that could lead to improved success. Interestingly the district suspended use of that apparently successful text series for reasons unknown. Follow-up (qualitative) discussions with the faculty and administration of this school confirmed that the staff was sorry to see this particular math series replaced as they strongly believed that it contributed to gains in student achievement (this school's mastery tests had experienced the greatest improvement among the Hartford elementary schools during this time period). Thus, we can see that displaying large volumes of complex data as graphs can assist in the decision-making process and leads to exploration of potentially rich new areas of inquiry.

Summary

This chapter explored the two main purposes of longitudinal analyses: to determine reasons that might explain current performance levels so that instructional improvements can be made, and second, to help predict future performance, thereby setting targets for future performance through benchmarking. The examples used can be carried out by any school to identify areas of improvement and to plan interventions. Additional examples and cases of improvement can be found at the University Council of Educational Administration (UCES) Web site (see Cases at http://www.ucea.org/cases/V2-Iss3/rolling.html) where data are used in several of these cases for analysis and decision-making.

We know that organizational improvement requires a deep understanding of past and present performance benchmarked to comparison school districts or standards. By drilling back in time as we did in the examples used in this chapter, reasonable and focused performance targets can be established that will help school staff make successful interventions.

Notes

1. Vasant Dhar and Roger Stein, *Seven Methods for Transforming Corporate Data into Business Intelligence* (Upper Saddle River, N.J.: Prentice Hall, 1997).

2. Joel A. Barker, *The Business of Paradigms*, video (Burnsville, Minn.: Charthouse International Learning Corporation, 1990).

3. W. H. Inmon, *Building the Data Warehouse*, second edition (New York: John Wiley & Sons, 1996).

4. Dhar and Stein, *Seven Methods*.

5. Edward R. Tufte, *Visual Explanations: Images and Quantities, Evidence and Narrative* (Cheshire, Conn.: Graphics Press, 1997).

6. Edward R. Tufte, *The Visual Display of Quantitative Information* (Cheshire, Conn.: Graphics Press, 1983).

7. Victoria L. Bernhardt, *Data Analysis for Comprehensive Schoolwide Improvement* (Larchmont, N.Y.: Eye on Education, 1998).

8. Ruth S. Johnson, *Setting Our Sights: Measuring Equity in School Change* (Los Angeles, Calif.: Achievement Council, 1996).

~

CHAPTER THREE

Equity Issues and Analyses

One of the most significant issues facing the nation today is ensuring educational equity. Specifically, this chapter focuses on the equity agenda as it applies to school improvement—identifying groups disadvantaged in educational achievement and planning interventions to correct those inequities. There are equity issues that are beyond the scope of this chapter, most notably equity in school funding and its impact on educational opportunity. While fiscal resources are no doubt critically important to school success, this book focuses on what educators can do with the resources at hand; thus, I will focus on the identification of disadvantaged populations within our schools and how to plan instructional interventions to correct those inequities. Therefore, the purpose of performing equity analyses, as used here, is to conduct internal and external scanning to identify areas of achievement inequity for improvement.

National Perspective

Equity 2000 is a national program addressing all issues that impact the disadvantaged and limit educational opportunity. The College Board embarked on the program, an ambitious initiative to increase the number of students from minority and disadvantaged groups who enter and succeed in post-secondary education. The College Board states "*Equity 2000* is a research-based, field-developed, district-wide, K–12 reform initiative. The goal of the program is to close the gap in the college-going and success rates between minority and non-minority, advantaged and disadvantaged students through a series of efforts, including the elimination of student tracking policies."[1] Educational equity has been broadly defined as the movement to close the achievement gap between groups in our society. Research on equity has tackled a number of areas, including ability grouping, gender, race, and ethnicity.

The most comprehensive volume describing procedures for equity analyses is Ruth Johnson's book *Setting Our Sights: Measuring Equity in School Change.*[2] Johnson's work covers a range of educational achievement issues looking at trend data largely using frequency analyses coupled with qualitative inquiry. Rather than duplicate Johnson's fine work, this chapter briefly addresses the use of graphs and charts (using frequency data) for identifying inequities, but then it focuses more fully on the disaggregation of data by searching for group differences. These differences can be identified by relatively uncomplicated statistical analyses.

Internal and External Scanning to Identify Areas of Inequality for Improvement: The Difference between Aggregate and Detail Data

Internal and external scanning are techniques used in the strategic planning process to help understand the environment within which the organization functions. If one school or school district is doing a better job among similar schools or school districts with at-risk students, it's important to recognize this limitation and plan for improvements. When certain populations of students are underperforming as compared with the general school population, this too is an area for intervention. Thus, the very process of searching for inequities, whether compared to external or internal organizations (or standards), is organizational scanning.

When we compare our school or district to others, we are often limited to aggregate frequency data (as this is generally the only available data) restricting our analyses to trends over time displayed in charts or graphs. This is because we do not have access to "detail" student data (individual student scores) from other school districts—all we have is a total score, generally reported as "percent of students" at some standard or the "average percentile ranking" of students in that school. As Johnson and others have pointed out, these trend analyses yield important information about how our school is doing overall. But when we are scanning internally and when detailed data are available, we can use powerful statistical analyses to help us better understand the nature and scope of group differences. Access to student detail data will allow us to "test" for statistically and practically important group differences.

What Is Data Disaggregation?

Data disaggregation is the separation of data by subgroup for analysis to determine if meaningful differences exist between and among those groups. When we only have access to total scores reported, such as total percent mastered or average percentile ranking, our analyses are limited to the use of frequency analyses, that is, looking at these "aggregate" scores over time displayed in a table or graph. Examples are shown in Tables 3.1 and 3.2.

Using these tables, we are disaggregating achievement data that have been reported as the percent of the school population that falls into each of two or four quartile bands, by gender and over time, and displaying these data in a simple table. But when we have each and every student's score, as provided on a data disk from a testing company, we can drill deeper into the dataset to see if differences exist that are both statistically and practically important.

For example, lets say that you find the average score for girls is at the 67th national percentile and that the boys are performing (average) at the 61st national percentile. At first glance you would want to address the boys' apparently lower performance, especially if that trend was consistent over three or more years. But is this difference statistically significant and important? It could be that "actual" performance is more equal and that this "truth" is masked by the nature of the reporting variable—national percentiles (see the discussion in chapter two on percent versus percentiles). If the difference was wider, such as 77th national percentile for girls and 60th national percentile for boys, then we probably could assume that the difference is real (using fast-track evaluation logic) and proceed to intervention. There is one other feasible scenario, though. It is entirely possible for almost equal "average"

Table 3.1   Data Disaggreggation: Female vs. Male Performance

	Female	Male	Difference
Year 1: Grade Level 6			
50th to 99th percentile	35	45	−10
1st to 49th percentile	65	55	10
Difference	−30	−10	
Year 2: Grade Level 6			
50th to 99th percentile	40	50	−10
1st to 49th percentile	60	50	10
Difference	−20	0	
Year 3: Grade Level 6			
50th to 99th percentile	45	60	−15
1st to 49th percentile	55	40	15
Difference	−10	20	

Table 3.2   Data Disagreggation by Quartile: Male vs. Female Performance

	Female	Male	Difference
Year 1: Grade Level 6			
76th to 99th percentile	15	20	5
51st to 75th percentile	20	25	5
26th to 50th percentile	35	30	−5
1st to 25th percentile	30	25	−5
Year 2: Grade Level 6			
76th to 99th percentile	20	25	5
51st to 75th percentile	20	25	5
26th to 50th percentile	40	30	−10
1st to 25th percentile	20	20	0
Year 3: Grade Level 6			
76th to 99th percentile	20	30	10
51st to 75th percentile	25	30	5
26th to 50th percentile	40	25	−15
1st to 25th percentile	15	15	0

scores between groups to be "proven" statistically different. That's because very large datasets can yield statistically significant results that are practically insignificant. Only statistical techniques and proper interpretation can uncover the true nature and scope of these differences. Finally, we must ask whether these differences, if found to be statistically significant, are practically important. That is, are the differences large enough to warrant taking action (which is a judgment call)? These are the issues that will be addressed in this chapter.

Data Disaggregation of Aggregate
Student Performance Measures

Table 3.1 provides achievement data for males and females looking at two key issues: (1) how girls and boys do in the same grade from year to year showing percent of students in the top half and the bottom half of the class and (2) how boys and girls (same cohort) do across time by quartile. The goal in both cases is to look for fewer students in the bottom half of the class or the lower two quartiles with movement toward the top half of the class (since the comparison is with national rankings, not local groups). In addition to gender, we could disaggregate performance across many other variables such as race, socioeconomic status (usually expressed as the percent of students receiving free and reduced lunch), special education versus regular education, attendance rates, discipline rates, or by school—if these data are readily available. By charting these data over time we are better able to identify areas that might need intervention.

Graphing Results for Easier Interpretation

If these data are in detail electronic format they can be imported into a spreadsheet program and easily graphed. We could also simply create a graph in the spreadsheet using the raw aggregate data. Consider the following example.

The Shepherd School has been looking at equity among girls and boys in several instructional areas as part of a three-year strategic goal. Table 3.1 shows their student performance data for language arts on a nationally standardized test. These data are divided into the top and bottom half of the class—the percent of students in the Shepherd School who fall within the 1st to 49th national percentile and the percent of students falling within the 50th to 99th national percentile—over a three-year period, disaggregated (or separated) by gender. The data show that more girls fall into the lower half of the class than boys and also that greater improvement appears to have been made by boys over the three-year time period. These data are more easily viewed in a graph (created in a spreadsheet program) as in Figure 3.1.

Using a stacked bar chart/graph we can clearly see that although girls are doing better in 1999 than they were in 1997, their performance still lags behind the boys. But it's hard to figure out what to fix with data that display such a wide range of performance levels—in this case only the top and bottom halves of the class. Actions could be better planned if we could break these data down further into quartile ranges. Table 3.2 and Figure 3.2 present these same data but displayed in quartile ranges.

Now the problem becomes clearer as there are many more girls in the 25th to 49th quartile band than boys and fewer girls in the two top quartiles

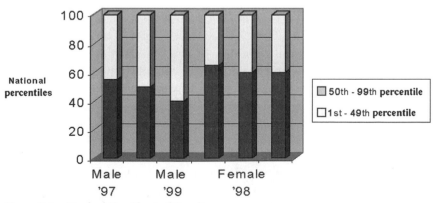

**Percent of Males & Females in Top/Bottom of Class
- Language Arts**

National percentiles

■ 50th - 99th percentile
□ 1st - 49th percentile

Male '97   Male '99   Female '98

Figure 3.1   Stacked Bar Chart of Results

Percent of Students in Each Quartile
Band - Language Arts

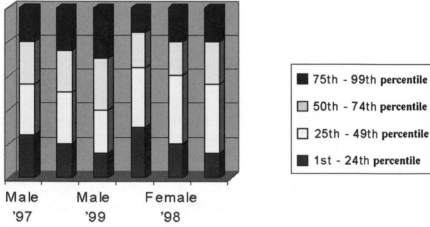

75th - 99th percentile

50th - 74th percentile

25th - 49th percentile

1st - 24th percentile

Male   Male   Female
'97   '99   '98

Figure 3.2   Stacked Bar Chart of Results

(75th–99th percentile and 50th–74th percentile). This school would, therefore, want to explore what instructional techniques and materials are being used with girls in these two data ranges. While continued overall improvement is needed, the school should be commended for an upward trend in performance for both boys and girls over this three-year time period. By disaggregating these data by quartile band across gender, school personnel have a much clearer picture of what needs specific attention.

Disaggregation across Many Variables for General Improvement

This has been only one example of the variables that can be reviewed for performance inequity. When data are available, equity can be reviewed by socioeconomic status, race, and ethnicity. We can also disaggregate data for other reasons, such as ensuring equity among schools, cohorts of students, attendance of students (do students who are more frequently absent also perform more poorly?), discipline (do students who are more frequently in trouble also perform more poorly?), and new students to the school. In each case we will be looking for areas of possible inequity to help plan for and drive instructional improvement.

The last category, whether new students to the school are pulling down scores and need special attention, is very interesting. In one of the districts in which I served as superintendent, staff were concerned that this was indeed the case and that special interventions were needed for these students to bring them up to the expected levels of performance. As a result of their concerns I disaggregated data by entrance date and found that new students to the school (within two years) actually had higher aggregate scores than those who had been with us for three years! Needless to say, the instructional changes took on a very different focus.

Testing for Group Differences—Drilling Down and Performing Powerful Statistical Analyses to Find the Real Problem

The examples discussed so far use frequency data displayed in a table or chart/graph for decision-making. But sometimes we will want to delve deeper into the data ("drill down") to determine if actual statistical differences exist between subject groups. To do so we will need to place the data into a statistics program and run special analyses—t-tests or analyses of variance. The following case study will demonstrate the importance of testing group means in this manner before taking action.

A set of student performance data has been entered into a spreadsheet from the North Middle School's 1999 administration of a statewide mastery test (see chapter 7 for a discussion of data extraction, transformation, and loading). The dataset is displayed in Figure 3.3 and includes two variables

	A	B	C	D	E	F	G	H	I	J	K
	Stud_ID	Last_Name	First_Name	Gender	Ethnicity	Math_Tot	Math_Com	Meth_Con	Reading	Leng_Arts	Writi
2	1169	Any Student	Any Student	1	5	23	9	76	31	67	
3	1027	Any Student	Any Student	1	9	31	76	75	68	8	
4	1054	Any Student	Any Student	1	8	25	75	67	62	75	
5	1100	Any Student	Any Student	1	7	28	40	7	53	83	
6	1222	Any Student	Any Student	1	8	34	99	26	31	42	
7	1029	Any Student	Any Student	1	4	35	79	54	88	8	
8	1407	Any Student	Any Student	1	6	30	53	98	1	80	
9	1394	Any Student	Any Student	1	9	20	6	61	25	40	
10	1210	Any Student	Any Student	1	9	22	24	40	39	13	
11	1033	Any Student	Any Student	1	2	24	4	78	45	41	
12	1107	Any Student	Any Student	1	5	18	94	33	55	1	
13	1468	Any Student	Any Student	1	5	31	78	96	56	35	
14	1204	Any Student	Any Student	1	7	33	42	13	79	97	
15	1142	Any Student	Any Student	1	3	29	67	78	72	68	
16	1148	Any Student	Any Student	1	7	31	24	71	17	38	
17	1355	Any Student	Any Student	1	6	28	69	86	9	79	
18	1460	Any Student	Any Student	1	4	29	30	89	81	12	
19	1389	Any Student	Any Student	1	4	17	44	47	19	27	
20	1073	Any Student	Any Student	1	6	20	60	35	32	42	
21	1423	Any Student	Any Student	1	7	31	20	98	38	36	
22	1131	Any Student	Any Student	1	2	34	46	70	6	11	
23	1214	Any Student	Any Student	1	9	25	25	41	72	6	
24	1116	Any Student	Any Student	1	3	22	4	11	56	21	
25	1047	Any Student	Any Student	1	3	27	90	82	80	92	
26	1406	Any Student	Any Student	1	3	30	46	49	19	60	

Figure 3.3   Detail Raw Data

Average Math Total Raw Scores

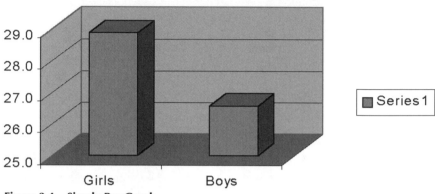

Figure 3.4   Simple Bar Graph

around which equity issues can be explored—gender and ethnicity—for student achievement scores in math, reading, writing, and language. In this example, staff at North Middle School want to know if there are group differences between boys and girls in math (this example will only explore gender, but the exploration of ethnicity is also important and the steps below could easily be duplicated for this analysis as well).

As a first step we can simply place the average total math raw score (from the standardized test) for girls and boys into a graph, as shown in Figure 3.4. (Note: This graph was created in a spreadsheet after finding the average for each group [disaggregated by gender], coded as girls = 1 and boys = 2 in the data chart above.)

Drilling Down with Statistical Techniques

We can see from the graph that the girls appear to be doing much better than the boys until we notice that there is only a 2.5-point spread (out of a possible 42 points) between the two groups. (If the graph had a zero base on the y axis, the 2.5 point difference would not be so pronounced.) It would be wise to test these group means for statistical significance before we jump to any conclusions. This requires running an "analysis of variance" test on the data, as this can tell us if the difference between the average scores of girls and boys is statistically significant. If you were testing ethnicity across three or more variables you would use an analysis of variance with a follow-up "post-hoc" analysis to identify statistically significant differences between and among the various groups.

While you can do analyses of variance (ANOVA) in some spreadsheet programs, it is often a tedious job to format the columns properly, so I prefer to use a good, inexpensive, and user-friendly statistics program—many of which are commercially available for around $100 (some of the more sophisticated programs cost upwards of $2,000, but for general use, the simpler programs work fine). Most of these programs allow you to easily move data back and forth between popular spreadsheet programs.

Interpreting Statistical Significance

Table 3.3 shows the ANOVA table for the mean differences between girls and boys for the total math score. We can see that the boys' average (group 2) was 26.55, while the girls (group 1) achieved an average of 28.86. At first glance, this apparent difference of a little over 2 points (on a scale of 42 points) would not be considered significant until we run the analysis of variance and find that the difference *is* statistically significant between the groups as shown by F-ratio and probability at p = .0014 (this value is *far less than* the required < .01 value denoting statistical significance between the group means). Thus, we could now conclude that there is apparent gender bias in the math program as evidenced from these data, although not what might have been expected, as girls are performing better than boys. But we do not know the scope of the statistical difference or the bias. Is this finding important enough to warrant action, that is, to place this issue ahead of other priorities that will take up valuable time and resources?

We are concerned here about the difference between "statistical" and "practical" significance. Sometimes small *mean* differences such as these (2 points on a 42-point scale) can show statistically significant results due to the

Table 3.3   Analysis of Variance Results: Boys vs. Girls for Mathematics

Dependent Variable = Math Total
Group Code Variable = Sex
N1 = 435   Mean Group 1 = 28.85977
N2 = 393   Mean Group 2 = 26.54962

ANOVA Summary Table					
Source	*Sum Sqres*	*df*	*Mean Sqres*	*F-Ratio*	*Prob*
Between Groups	1101.87544	1	1101.87544	10.26865	.0014
Within Groups	88633.72842	826	107.30476		
Total	89735.60386	827			

sheer size of the sample—in this example 828 cases, or 435 girls and 393 boys. Jessica Utts[3] notes that:

> You should be aware that "statistical significance" does not mean the two variables have a relationship that you would necessarily consider to be of practical importance. For example, a table based on a very large number of observations will have little trouble achieving the title of statistical significance even if the relationship between the two variables is only minor. On the other hand, an interesting relationship in a population may fail to achieve statistical significance in the sample if there are only a few observations. It is hard to rule out chance unless you have either a very strong relationship or a sufficiently large sample.

In the present example we have a relatively large number of cases that has been found to have a statistical difference between the groups. Thus, we might conclude that something important is going on; that is, we should not dismiss the finding at this point, but we are still not able to focus in on just what is contributing to the statistically significant findings. We could determine that, given the large number of cases, this statistically significant result lacks practical importance. But lets explore further.

What Does This All Mean?

To understand the nature of the difference between the groups we need to understand the nature of analyses of variance. Lets take one last look at these data before we make any final decisions on follow-up actions.

It would be useful to chart/graph the boys' and girls' scores on a histogram that shows how many individuals achieved each score point. Using a simple statistics program we can also overlay the normal curve to show what would be expected in a "normal" population. In this way we can determine if the groups, either boys or girls, differ significantly from what would be normally expected. Most statistics programs can easily create histograms (along with a number of other graph types), and we will instruct the program to overlay the normal curve over each group's performance data. The results are shown in Figures 3.5 and 3.6.

These graphs tell us two very important things about the students' group scores. First, we can see that both groups tend to do slightly better overall than what would normally be expected (note the numbers of students performing above the mid-point on the normal curve overlay). That's good news. But more importantly, both graphs also show that many students lag behind the normal curve mid-point. These students are represented as bars to the left of the normal curve mid-point on each X-axis, particularly score ranges between 2 and 22. The boys have large subgroups at scores of 4 and 22, while the girls have a moderate number of individuals clustering at scores

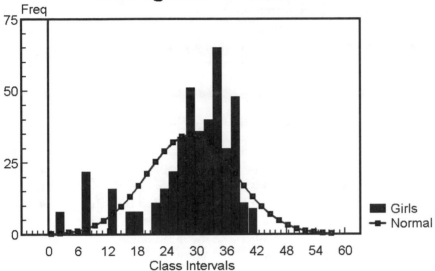

Figure 3.5   Histogram with Normal Curve Overlay Girls' Math Scores

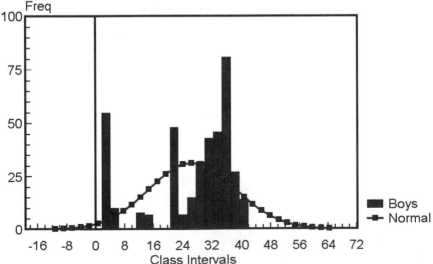

Figure 3.6   Histogram with Normal Curve Overlay Boys' Math Scores

8 and 14. These anomalies should be investigated further by talking to teachers to determine if anything unusual happened during testing, if large groups of students were absent during the year when important material was covered, and so on. However, if nothing unusual was occurring, then the instructional program warrants review. These anomalies caused the ANOVA to be statistically significant.

What Makes for Statistically Significant Results?

To summarize, we initially graphed the mean scores for each group and found what appeared to be a slight difference in mean scores. We then tested the girls and boys scores for statistical significance, finding that this small difference in the mean scores between groups was indeed statistically significant. At that point we were not sure whether this difference was practically important, given the sample size, because the mean difference between groups seemed so small—only 2 points on a 42-point scale. Then we looked further into the data, exploring the frequency with which boys and girls achieved each point using a histogram, and subsequently uncovered very important findings. We determined that, although each group performed slightly better than what would be normally expected overall, there were groups of students who scored much more poorly than the average *within* each group. *This dispersion of scores is why the analysis of variance turned out to be statistically significant.* Analyses of variance (and t-tests) are tests of variance around the mean, not simply of mean differences.

In this example, the histogram has shown us wide variance within each group, which the ANOVA picked up even with mean difference between groups so close to one another. And the differences were not simply due to large sample sizes as we can see in the histograms. Thus, this process of drilling down into the data has uncovered an important finding: there are groups of boys and girls that are indeed performing well below the average for the group—and school. *As a result, we may have uncovered achievement bias as contrasted to our original hypothesis of gender bias.* We would definitely want to follow up on these results and take a careful look at the instructional program for these potentially underperforming students.

Summary

A fundamental goal of our schools should be to provide equal opportunity for all children. Schools do not willfully deny students equal opportunity; rather, it is often an artifact of traditional approaches to education. Old attitudes toward girls' math achievement, instructional tracking, and racial biases all contribute to inequality and lack of opportunity. Special techniques are needed to identify and correct these problems. The *Equity 2000* "movement" is arguably the most effective sustained program to assist schools achieve equal access and opportunity for all children. The techniques and examples used in this chapter will help schools identify potential problems as a focus for interventions.

Notes

1. College Board, www.collegeboard.com, January 2000.

2. Ruth S. Johnson, *Setting Our Sights: Measuring Equity in School Change* (Los Angeles, Calif.: Achievement Council, 1996).

3. Jessica M. Utts, *Seeing through Statistics* (Boston, Mass.: Duxbury Press, 1996).

CHAPTER FOUR

~

Exploring the Local Landscape

Before setting off on a vacation with the family car, the first thing the experts tell us to do is check under the hood. So we check the oil, the water in the radiator, the battery, the windshield washer fluid, and so on, and off we go. As to our personal finances, once a year we are supposed to perform a financial checkup making sure that our expenses are in line with income and investments are yielding the proper return. And once a year we get our yearly physical as a routine check to see if all is well. These periodic checkups are helpful in determining if hidden problems exist that are in need of correction. In management, a popular form of supervision is "MBWA"—management by walking around. We don't expect to see problems, but we can learn much about how the organization functions, spotting potential problems through this regular checking-up process. Another way to think about this process is as an exploration to determine if there are any problems in need of our attention. When using fast-track evaluation it is useful to have checkups where and when we can to identify potential problems that are not readily apparent through standard reporting methods. Thus, this chapter is about exploring the local landscape to identify and solve problems that are otherwise hidden.

The "local landscape" is defined as the organization over which we have control and for which we have data. The purpose of exploring, then, is to identify areas in need of improvement through internal scanning. An example would be an inquiry into possible teacher grade inflation; for instance, are teachers' grades inflated as compared with related standardized measures (in the same subject matter area)? If they are, achievement will likely improve when grades (or local expectations) are brought more in line with these standards.

This raises the question as to what those standards are that should be used in curriculum alignment and grading. While the standards will most often be externally generated, such as math and language arts standards, state mastery tests, and so on, acceptable performance levels are almost always defined locally, at least in terms of student grading. For example, if the math standards in algebra call for solving quadratic equations (externally generated), the grading standards of students will be determined locally, that is, determining what constitutes an A. The important consideration is whether these external and internal standards are aligned. If students are mostly getting local grades of A in algebra, one assumes that they will be able to perform to this level on nationally ranked exams. The purpose of this chapter is to provide guidance on collecting and analyzing local data to address these important achievement issues.

Challenges to Conducting These Queries

Unlike the previous chapters where data were readily available and the comparisons were clearly understood, there are serious challenges here to conducting these analyses, specifically, determining appropriate comparison standards. Also challenging is the process of extraction, transformation, and loading (the data ETL process) of these data into some form of computer program for analysis. Moreover, the analyses themselves will be more complicated.

First among these challenges is determining the appropriate comparison of internal and external benchmarks. In the algebra example described above we would likely be able to find an external exam, keyed to national standards, to serve as an external benchmark that is already being administered in the district or school. And since math is so well understood and its objectives well mapped for testing, it will be easy (relatively speaking, as all of these tasks are fairly challenging) for us to match objectives between classroom work and the test for comparison purposes. But this is much more difficult in language arts, social studies, the sciences, or the arts. In fact, beyond the basic three Rs, testing is not very well developed, which makes these comparisons difficult, if not impossible, to achieve with any assurance of reliability (consistency) and validity (accuracy). As a result, the findings of these queries can at best be used as a window to a potential problem to be followed up by more in-depth analyses and discussions.

Another challenge is the gathering of data for multiple comparisons that are often needed to arrive at meaningful conclusions (known as the data extraction, transformation, and loading process). It's one thing to gather the data on our algebra example for a single class or two, but it's quite another task to gather data on all classes for many subject areas and then try to match those to some form of a test. The time typically spent on such comprehensive data gathering could not normally justify the ends. And when there is no clearly appropriate test (or measure) available for external benchmarking, what we are left to work with has to justify the time and energy spent on data ETL.

The Data Warehousing Environment

The natural result of these challenges is to render exploring a more practical tool when there is a data warehouse in place. Data warehousing, as discussed in chapter 8, is an emerging application in educational leadership. Data warehouses can contain all student data over multiple years, making these explorations easy to accomplish, often in just minutes. Thus, it will be useful to think of this chapter as a glimpse into the future of what becomes possible in a data warehousing environment. But to show what can be done without this technology, the chapter will conclude with a case study using everyday paper and pencil approaches and methods.

Using a Data Warehouse—Looking for Class Grades Alignment to Standardized Tests

The advantage of a data warehouse is that it provides access to data for conducting complex multiple queries—quickly and easily—as we will be doing in this example. In our grade alignment query we want to know if the grades earned/assigned in ninth-grade science classes are aligned with results in the tenth-grade science mastery test. Another view of this question is whether there is any evidence of under- or overinflated grades for this subject area. This could be important because anchoring class grades to standardized achievement can help with curriculum alignment and achievement.

In Connecticut a rigorous tenth-grade mastery test is administered to all students with a major subtest in science. Unfortunately, none of the earlier grade level mastery tests include a science component, and very few districts administer science achievement tests at earlier grade levels, so the challenge is to find a measure of science achievement that can be used as an early predictor and benchmark. A graduate student of mine recently took on this query/challenge, extracting all the needed data by hand, entering it into a sophisticated statistics program, and performing several analyses, including regression, to look for predictors of science achievement. The project took her an entire semester, with the vast majority of her time spent on data extraction, transformation, and loading into the statistics program. Her research question was whether there is a relationship between end of ninth-grade science class grades and the score achieved by these same students at the end of tenth grade on the science subtest of the Connecticut mastery test. To explore this analysis, I will use a commercially available data warehousing system and an actual district database.

The concept map for this problem is shown in Figure 4.1. Here we are simply matching up the grades received by students in ninth-grade earth science classes with the results on the end of the tenth-grade state mastery science test. Although there is not a one-for-one comparison here, that is, we do not have a specific and exclusive science test to match against the specific objectives covered in these classes, we can assume that this tenth-grade test includes objectives taken from the courses (known to be the case). This is easy to check by reviewing the learning objectives of the test; and in this case the test does include learning objectives in these content areas.

As to our hypothesis, we would assume at the very least that there would be a moderate correlation, or a relationship, between those students who do well in ninth-grade earth science classes and who also do well on the tenth-grade test. If there is misalignment, that is, if grades are over- or underinflated as compared to test results, then discussions should ensue with the teachers to determine what factors might be causing this misalignment. Should that turn out to be the case, it could simply be test/course objective misalignment (i.e., the specific objectives tested were not those taught). Then we would

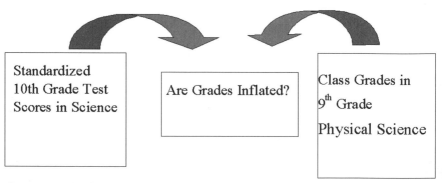

Grade Inflation

| Standardized 10th Grade Test Scores in Science | Are Grades Inflated? | Class Grades in 9th Grade Physical Science |

Figure 4.1　Simple Concept Map of the Query

not be concerned, and no action would be warranted. But if we expected alignment between class grades and the test because the curriculum and test objectives were fairly well matched and found test/class grade mismatch, we would want to have follow-up discussions with the teachers.

Using a data warehousing system I can quickly extract and graph the necessary data for the query. Figure 4.2 shows the graph of students' ninth-grade class grades in earth science (three difficulty levels) along with these same students' scores on the tenth-grade state mastery test in science (exported to a spreadsheet). The data show that students perform generally the same on the tenth-grade test regardless of course difficulty or class grades earned. Why would so many students across three course levels perform at generally the same level on the test, yet have such a wide range of class grades (A to F)? And, if Earth Science P7 is a more advanced class than Earth Science P5, why is there little apparent difference in standardized test scores between students in these classes? What about between and among the three levels of the course—P5, P6, and P7?

These questions cannot be answered by the computer system or statistical analyses alone. They can only be understood through open discussions with teachers, but the window to these issues is opened through the technology.

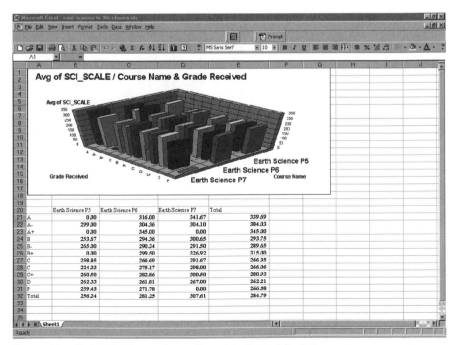

Figure 4.2 Data Warehouse Query Export to Spreadsheet Program

The value of these technologies is that this query and the needed analyses can be run in a matter of minutes, not the weeks it took for my graduate student. And, if we wanted to change the query from science classes and test scores to math or language arts, it's a simple matter of selecting different variables—again a matter of minutes. To run more sophisticated regression analyses, we can easily export the data from the data warehouse to a spreadsheet as shown in Figure 4.2. Then, it's a relatively simple matter to import the spreadsheet into a statistics program. The value of these emerging technologies is discussed more in depth in chapter 8, but their utility for "exploring the local landscape" can be readily seen here.

These queries were easy to run, thanks to the data warehousing system and the close alignment between test and course objectives. But when we move to other instructional areas, our confidence in the comparisons may diminish as the relationships become harder to justify. For example, this particular tenth-grade test includes an interdisciplinary learning area subtest—an area with no clear ninth- or tenth-grade class comparison. Yet, using the data warehouse, we could continue to explore a range of coursework that might contribute to the interdisciplinary performance area of the test. Thus, we could continue exploring the degree to which success in some of the ninth- and tenth-grade subject areas, such as algebra, freshman English, foreign languages, music, and so on, are related to success on this challenging test. But the further we stray from objective alignment between the test and the curriculum, the more these analyses become problematic, highly unreliable, and likely invalid. In the final analysis, the usable areas of inquiry that are possible in this environment are limited by the data available in the system and our ability to structure a meaningful (relatively reliable and valid) query.

With these technologies we could drill down further into the dataset to explore such questions as whether there is a relationship between course grades, standardized test scores, and participation in student activities. Or we could look at course-taking trends and relationship to grade point average (GPA) or standardized test scores. Once again, the only limits are having the necessary data loaded into the data warehouse and our ability to structure a meaningful query.

Case Study: Data from a State Report Card Does Not Always Tell the Whole Story

Many states now issue an annual report card on each district's and/or school's progress including data covering expenses, test scores, teacher/student ratios, minority enrollment, and the like. Figure 4.3 shows a small segment of one such report from a New York elementary school while Figure 4.4 shows part of the Austin, Texas, district report card. Although these report cards are of-

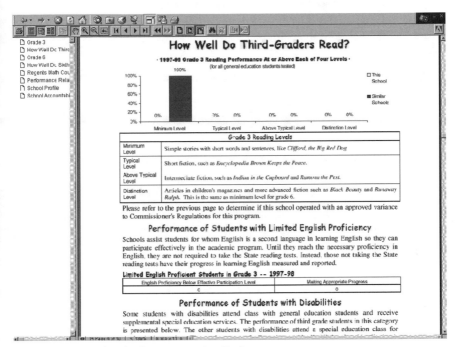

Figure 4.3   Sample District Report, New York

ten filled with interesting and useful data intended to inform the public, they sometimes do not tell the whole story, as this next example demonstrates. One such Connecticut report card (only partially shown here and for just one school covering 1996) is displayed in Figure 4.5.

Reviewing the data for all of the schools, the superintendent noted the following data for two of its elementary schools. Concerns in the district emerged regarding a comparison between the number of instructional hours in language arts and reading performance between the two schools. Here is the relevant data taken directly from the "report card" for this issue:

School 3 Estimated Hours of Instruction (Language Arts)   432
School 4 Estimated Hours of Instruction (Language Arts)   360

The language arts achievement levels of the two schools were reported as follows:

School 3 Reading (Percent Mastery)   73.7%
School 4 Reading (Percent Mastery)   63.0%

From these data it would appear that there is a relationship between hours spent on language arts instruction and the percent of students mastering the

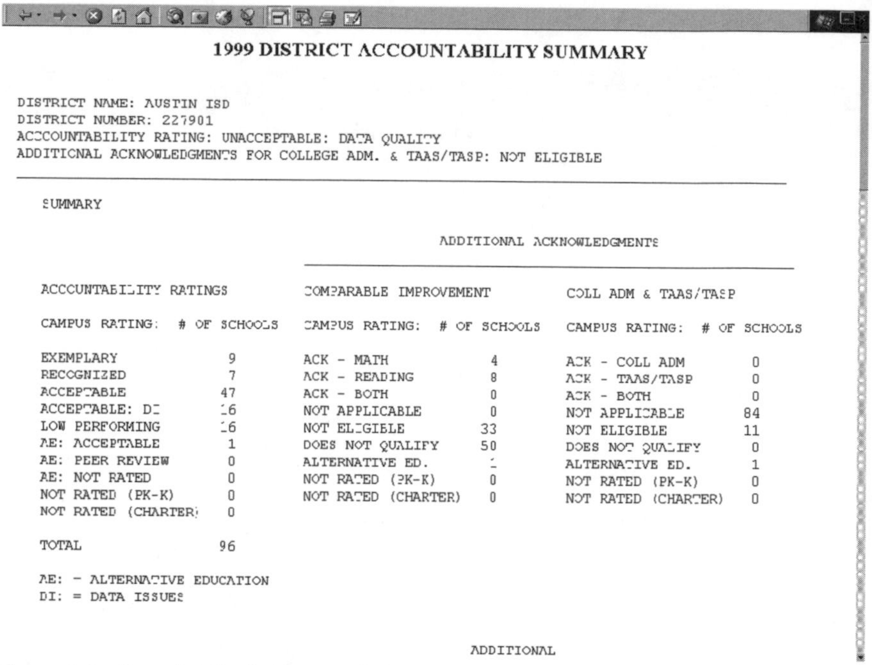

1999 DISTRICT ACCOUNTABILITY SUMMARY

DISTRICT NAME: AUSTIN ISD
DISTRICT NUMBER: 227901
ACCOUNTABILITY RATING: UNACCEPTABLE: DATA QUALITY
ADDITIONAL ACKNOWLEDGMENTS FOR COLLEGE ADM. & TAAS/TASP: NOT ELIGIBLE

SUMMARY

ADDITIONAL ACKNOWLEDGMENTS

ACCOUNTABILITY RATINGS		COMPARABLE IMPROVEMENT		COLL ADM & TAAS/TASP	
CAMPUS RATING:	# OF SCHOOLS	CAMPUS RATING:	# OF SCHOOLS	CAMPUS RATING:	# OF SCHOOLS
EXEMPLARY	9	ACK - MATH	4	ACK - COLL ADM	0
RECOGNIZED	7	ACK - READING	8	ACK - TAAS/TASP	0
ACCEPTABLE	47	ACK - BOTH	0	ACK - BOTH	0
ACCEPTABLE: DI	16	NOT APPLICABLE	0	NOT APPLICABLE	84
LOW PERFORMING	16	NOT ELIGIBLE	33	NOT ELIGIBLE	11
AE: ACCEPTABLE	1	DOES NOT QUALIFY	50	DOES NOT QUALIFY	0
AE: PEER REVIEW	0	ALTERNATIVE ED.	1	ALTERNATIVE ED.	1
AE: NOT RATED	0	NOT RATED (PK-K)	0	NOT RATED (PK-K)	0
NOT RATED (PK-K)	0	NOT RATED (CHARTER)	0	NOT RATED (CHARTER)	0
NOT RATED (CHARTER)	0				
TOTAL	96				

AE: - ALTERNATIVE EDUCATION
DI: = DATA ISSUES

ADDITIONAL

Figure 4.4 Sample District Report, Texas

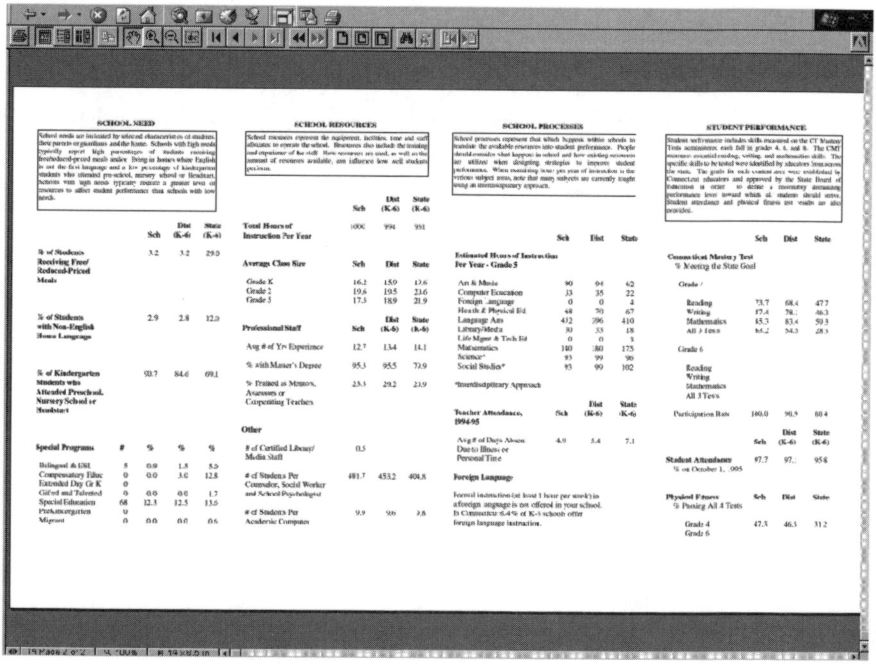

SCHOOL NEED

	Sch	Dist (K-6)	State (K-6)
% of Students Receiving Free/ Reduced-Priced Meals	3.2	3.2	29.5
% of Students with Non-English Home Language	2.9	2.8	12.9
% of Kindergarten Students who Attended Preschool, Nursery School or Headstart	93.7	84.6	69.1

Special Programs	#	%	%	%
Bilingual & ESL	5	0.9	1.5	5.5
Compensatory Educ	0	0.0	3.0	12.8
Extended Day Gr K	0			
Gifted and Talented	0	0.0	0.0	1.7
Special Education	68	12.3	12.5	13.6
Prekindergarten	0			
Migrant	0	0.0	0.0	0.6

SCHOOL RESOURCES

	Sch	Dist (K-6)	State (K-6)
Total Hours of Instruction Per Year	1000	994	991

Average Class Size	Sch	Dist	State
Grade K	16.2	15.9	19.6
Grade 2	19.6	19.5	23.6
Grade 5	17.5	18.9	21.9

Professional Staff	Sch	Dist (K-6)	State (K-6)
Avg # of Yrs Experience	12.7	13.4	14.1
% with Master's Degree	95.3	95.5	79.9
% Trained as Mentors, Assessors or Cooperating Teachers	23.3	29.2	23.9

Other	Sch	Dist	State
# of Certified Library/ Media Staff	0.5		
# of Students Per Counselor, Social Worker and School Psychologist	481.7	453.2	404.8
# of Students Per Academic Computer	9.9	9.6	9.8

SCHOOL PROCESSES

Estimated Hours of Instruction Per Year - Grade 5	Sch	Dist	State
Art & Music	90	94	62
Computer Education	33	35	22
Foreign Language	0	0	4
Health & Physical Ed	68	70	67
Language Arts	432	396	410
Library/Media	30	33	18
Life Mgmt & Tech Ed	0	0	3
Mathematics	140	180	175
Science*	93	99	96
Social Studies*	93	99	102

*Interdisciplinary Approach

Teacher Attendance, 1994-95	Sch	Dist (K-6)	State (K-6)
Avg # of Days Absent Due to Illness or Personal Time	4.9	5.4	7.1

Foreign Language

Formal instruction (at least 1 hour per week) in a foreign language is not offered in your school. In Connecticut 6.4% of K-5 schools offer foreign language instruction.

STUDENT PERFORMANCE

Connecticut Mastery Test % Meeting the State Goal	Sch	Dist	State
Grade 4			
Reading	73.7	68.4	47.7
Writing	87.4	78.1	46.3
Mathematics	85.3	83.4	59.3
All 3 Tests	65.2	54.3	28.3
Grade 6			
Reading			
Writing			
Mathematics			
All 3 Tests			
Participation Rate	100.0	98.9	88.4

	Sch	Dist (K-6)	State (K-6)
Student Attendance % on October 1, 1995	97.7	97.1	95.8

Physical Fitness % Passing All 4 Tests	Sch	Dist	State
Grade 4	47.3	46.5	31.2
Grade 6			

Figure 4.5 Sample School Report

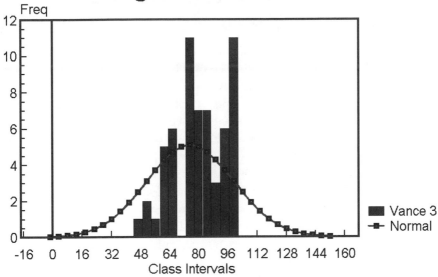

Figure 4.6   Frequencies of Verbal Ability Scores, School 3

state reading test. This anomaly was a surprise to the superintendent as he reviewed his district's "report card," which prompted a review by the principals and other staff to look into the issue and make necessary adjustments if warranted.

The first thing administrators did was confirm the number of instructional hours reported as accurate. After a review of reading and language arts instructional time and reporting procedures, it was determined that the "report cards" were accurate. Once they were sure that a simple reporting error had not been the cause of the anomaly and that the actual number of instructional hours between these two schools was genuinely different, the staff began looking at the impact that this and several other issues could have on the reading scores. Since the percent of students mastering the test between schools also appeared to be significantly different, they felt that something real was going on that needed further review. Was it simply a matter of asking school 4 to spend more time on reading or was there something more going on here?

The district had just completed a review of its language arts and reading programs a few years earlier and had put a fairly rigorous monitoring system in place that led them to dismiss curriculum and instructional practices as the cause. In one of their discussions a teacher raised the question as to whether students were of equal ability, noting that students in school 4 appeared to be more needy than in recent years. Dismissing differences in instructional techniques as major contributing factors, the staff decided to look at the student ability variable more closely. Fortunately, this school district had been administering a high-performance standardized test that included both verbal and quantitative ability scores. The staff decided to enter the relevant data for all the students into a statistics program and ran an analysis of covariance to see if ability was a strong contributing factor for the poorer performance of students in school 4. Analyses of covariance use an independent variable, in this case ability, to equate scores before running the analysis. Thus, the analysis helps to isolate the effect of a particular variable, ability, on the dependent variable, reading.

It works much the same way as handicapping does in golf. The Professional Golfing Association's (PGA) handicapping system, for example, puts me on a more even playing field with better players by equalizing our scores from the outset. Thus, I can be a lousy golfer (let the truth be known!), but I can still outscore a better player by turning in a round of 90 with a handicap of 28 (assuming I had a really good day!) as compared to his score of 80 with a handicap of 2. It's the same general principle used in equalizing an achievement score (in the present case reading) based on a relevant variable (verbal ability) to better determine if the isolated variable (ability) has an impact on learning. To run these analyses, the data from a spreadsheet have been read into a more powerful statistics program. Table 4.1 shows the results.

The first thing we notice is that the average score for each elementary school is much closer to one another than the percent mastered as reported in the district/school profile. And school 4 actually has an average reading score *higher* than school 3!

	Reading % Mastered	Reading Avg. Score
School 3	73.7	71.05
School 4	63.0	72.35

How can this be? This apparent disparity between *percent* of students' reading mastery and *average* reading score could easily occur if a large number of students in school 4 had just missed the mastery cut-off score. Looking at the percent of students achieving mastery alone can be misleading and misrepresent what is actually happening with achievement because anyone under the cut-off score, no matter how close, would not be counted in the score. We should also note that the analysis of variance was statistically significant, meaning that (1) there is a

Table 4.1   Analysis of Variance for School Differences

Between-Subjects Factors

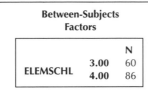

		N
ELEMSCHL	3.00	60
	4.00	86

Descriptive Statistics
Dependent Variable: DRP UNIT

School Averges →

ELEMSCHL	Mean	Std. Deviation	N
3.00	71.05	10.76	60
4.00	72.35	10.36	06
Total	71.82	10.51	146

Tests of Between-Subjects Effects
Dependent Variable: DQP UNIT

Source	Type III Sum of Squares	df	Mean Square	F	Sig.
Corrected Model	7639.218(a)	2	3819.109	63.297	.000
Intercept	4462.817	1	4452.817	76.303	.000
VANCE	7570.596	1	7570.596	129.575	.000
ELEMSCHL	516.615	1	516.615	0.033	.000
Error	8363.789	143	58488		
Total	768983.000	146			
Corrected Total	16002.007	145			

R Squared = .477 (Adjusted R Squared = .470)

Significance factors for school, verbal ability (VANCE), and the corrected model

difference in achievement between elementary schools and (2) there is also a statistically significant difference in verbal ability scores (expressed as VANCE for verbal ability, normal curve equivalent (NCE) scores). Checking the average verbal ability scores for each school yields the following:

School 3 mean verbal ability NCE score   80.3
School 4 mean verbal ability NCE score   75.3

Testing these means for significance using the analysis of variance, we find that the mean scores are statistically significant at the < .03 level (computed separately but not shown), indicating that the verbal ability levels of the students between schools probably have some practical significance and are impacting the overall results.

Putting all of this data together we can get a clearer picture of what is taking place at each school:

	Reading Percent Mastered	Reading Mean (Avg.) Score	Verbal Ability Mean NCE Score
School 3	73.7	71.05	80.3
School 4	63.0	72.35	75.3

School 3, with a verbal ability mean score of 80.3, has, on average, more able students than school 4 (meaning they have a higher ability level in the verbal areas). The fact that the average reading score for school 4 is actually *higher* than school 3 is not surprising when we look at a histogram of the verbal ability scores shown in Figures 4.6 and 4.7. School 4 has a greater dispersion of verbal ability scores around the mean that could easily account for a slightly higher average score caused primarily by the students skewed to the right on the histogram. School 4 could at the same time have a lower percentage of students achieving mastery, caused by the skewing of students below the average and below the arbitrary state determined cut-off score for mastery.

Given all of this new data, should the superintendent and staff be concerned about the apparent disparity in achievement between the two schools

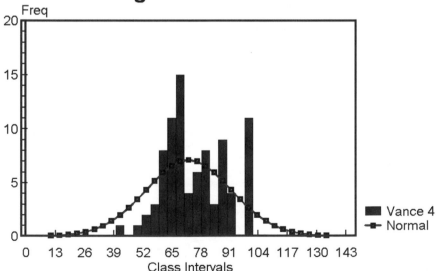

Figure 4.7   Frequencies of Verbal Ability Scores, School 4

as first reported and published on the state district/school "report card"? No, because we can now see that school 4, which had a lower percentage of students mastering the test, also has a group of less able students who must have just missed the cut-off score for achieving mastery. School 4 certainly would want to follow up and continue working with these youngsters, but there is no need for alarm as the original reported data would signal.

This process of drilling down further into the available data yields new and important findings. Had the staff taken the state district/school "report card" at face value, they would have concluded, erroneously, that there was a deficiency in instructional hours at school 4 resulting in poorer reading achievement. That would have been a reasonable conclusion given the data that were reported and published. But as we have seen, results can be reported using many different scores, each with more or less meaning (i.e., representing the full picture), thereby potentially leading to misleading conclusions. For example, the juxtaposition of reported hours spent in reading with the percent of students reaching an arbitrary cut-off mastery score presents an erroneous picture in this case. The more revealing data were the verbal ability scores (not included on the report card) as they relate to average reading score and the percent of students achieving reading mastery. The analyses of covariance technique revealed that the verbal ability scores were having an impact on achievement, putting school 4 at a slight disadvantage as compared to its sister school. And a further display of these scores using histograms showed us the probable reason school 4 had fewer students achieving mastery—the clustering of a large group of students below the average. If any action were to be taken, school 4 should be commended for its level of achievement and encouraged to keep working with these children to help them achieve mastery.

Summary

Of all the frames for conducting fast-track evaluation, "exploring the local landscape" may be the most dependent upon emerging technologies such as data warehousing. We have seen that the main purpose of exploring is internally scanning the performance of our organization to search for areas in need of improvement that might not be readily apparent. For example, grade inflation, if it exists, will not serve the needs of students, and it is in everyone's interest to match expectations between coursework, grades, and standardized measures whenever possible. One of the greatest frustrations parents often have is not understanding how their child can do so well in school, yet not so well on the state mastery test or some nationally normed test. This problem can range from a simple misinterpretation of a reported score to a misaligned curriculum. We have also seen how reliability and validity become a concern in making these comparisons and matches, but it behooves us to search for congruence wherever it makes sense to do so and is technically feasible. No doubt, however, making defensible matches and comparisons is a challenge; one should be wary of the cautions and problems inherent in the analyses. Regardless, I would encourage the making of such comparisons because having this information, albeit with its flaws and limitations, is inevitably better than operating blindly.

Another challenge to conducting exploring with any regularity is easy access to all the data needed. The solution to this challenge is the data warehouse. These emerging technologies and their use will be discussed in chapter 8.

Finally, we saw an example of how some basic information, no matter how well intended, can be seriously misinterpreted without additional drilling down to uncover the root causes of a difference in achievement scores. In the case of the two elementary schools, staff were able to conduct this analysis using everyday tools such as simple spreadsheet and statistics programs. True—it was a lot of work, but there was a lot at stake, which made the effort worthwhile. It is an example of not accepting at face value what the published data tell us, but rather using our informed intuition to guide our deeper inquiry. Without doing so, erroneous results would be validated and, worse, improper actions might be taken. When warranted by the level of concern, it's important to drill down until we have exhausted all practical steps before taking action. Doing so in this case study led to a commendation rather than an indictment. Had the mistake been left unchallenged, morale and achievement could have been seriously impacted.

Although difficult and sometimes time consuming, exploring can be one of the most powerful analytical tools at the disposal of school leaders and staff (second perhaps only to longitudinal analyses for setting improvement targets). Despite the work needed, I have found that the impact is almost always significant and worth the time invested.

~

CHAPTER FIVE

Budgetary Control and Reallocation: Finding the Resources to Meet New Needs

Where will we find the resources to implement the changes discussed throughout this book? Financial resources are critical to the success of any organization and, in schools, we know that these resources are finite and limited. The era of large annual budget increases to pay for new programs is long, over resulting in budgets that are being squeezed tighter and tighter. Creative budgeting can just take us so far, as the lion's share of budgets now regularly go for generally fixed costs such as salaries, benefits, and buildings. These pressures require that school administrators practice two key budgetary concepts: budgetary control and budgetary reallocation. Budgetary control is simply oversight and management of the budget to control expenses and maintain a balanced budget. Budget overruns, unless caused by extremely unusual events/expenses, are not viewed favorably by town and city finance authorities and can seriously erode their confidence in the superintendent. Hence, budgetary control takes on even more importance than just fiscal control—it is often seen as an indication of the school administration's ability to run the school system.

Budgetary reallocation becomes necessary as a technique to identify existing funds for new programs. It is a way to reallocate financial resources to meet current organizational needs. As funds for new programs are very difficult to come by in most school budgets, we need ways to identify resources from existing programs that may not be needed as much as a new program initiative to meet pressing demands. For example, if the district decided it needed to replace its elementary reading program, it would be difficult in most districts to secure all the necessary funds in one budget year, as new text-book adoptions are a good deal more expensive than yearly textbook mainte-nance budgets would allow. But by reviewing the budget to free up funds from accounts that might not be so pressing, experience tells us that the needed funds (or a good portion or those needed funds) can often be identified. This would not likely hold true for a new program startup (such as adding a string music program or a gifted and talented program) that will incur yearly (on-going) additional expenses. In such cases, budget reallocations would have to be permanent, which require more difficult decisions regarding budget allo-cations from the town/city financing authority. Regardless, *some* funds can generally be identified for reallocation through these techniques. The pur-pose of this chapter is to review these two important budgeting strategies and to provide operational examples of how they can be carried out.

The techniques presented in this chapter were taught to me by Gary Franzi (franzi@snet.net), a colleague and friend. Franzi is an expert in school finance and taught me most of what I've learned about finance. He holds a BS and an MBA with specialization in economics, finance, accounting, and business strategy and has had coursework at some of the nation's top business schools, including Harvard, Stanford, The Wharton School, and Dartmouth. He has worked in the private sector serving as chief financial officer and di-rector of corporate communications and as director and budget officer for corporate finance at Traveler's Corporation. He currently serves as director of finance at the Avon (CT) public schools, where I had the good fortune to work with him for a time. The ideas and concepts that follow are examples of how he develops and manages the budget, and I am grateful to him for sharing his expertise to help round out this book. School improvement and the related strategies and tactics discussed throughout this book are impor-tant, but so, too, are finding the resources to implement change. Franzi pro-vides us with proven strategies for success.

What Is Budgetary Control and Reallocation and How Is It Conducted?

There is an important connection between budgetary control and realloca-tion that may not be readily apparent. By going through the process of budg-etary reallocation, we are able to establish a solid benchmark or basis for the following year's budget that ensures better control as that new budget is im-plemented. Hence, these two topics are very much related and must be con-sidered part of one strategy to manage the budget and to find dollars among existing allocations to fund important new initiatives.

In developing a budget Franzi asks the following questions: First, where did you underspend last year? Then, where did you overspend and why? Were there any unplanned events, or did cost overruns occur due to a lack of appropriate controls in a specific area of the budget or organization? Knowing *why* spending was up or down for each line item is critical to knowing how to build the following year's budget. This process establishes a *baseline plan* for the coming year. Franzi reminds us that it is hard to know where your organization is headed without understanding where it has been. We have used this same basic technique to determine a baseline of student performance to set improvement targets in chapter 2. The universal technique is applied here to help us understand and control the budget.

Once the baseline plan is established for the budget, Franzi makes adjustments for the subsequent year plan based on program and operational and staff needs, along with inflationary adjustments, on all key accounts. This yields a revised baseline. Finally, he determines where there are opportunities for reallocation by reassigning some of the dollars from each line item that had a surplus the previous year to meet new priorities. If needed, new initiatives are then added to the budget. This process establishes the budget proposal for the next year. The key point here is that, by following this process, we have established a reliable baseline for understanding and justifying the budget and any needed increases. Franzi cautions against taking any aspect of the budget for granted, saying that no stone should be left unturned in trying to find opportunities for reallocation and savings. The key is to ensure that the budget adequately funds programs at levels to attain desired student performance objectives.

There are other opportunities that may exist to identify funds within current allocations for reallocation to new needs. For example, Franzi argues that we should not take for granted such expenditures as transportation contracts, facility maintenance costs, copier costs, and food services contracts. In one case, Franzi was able to renegotiate his transportation contract to save in excess of 20 percent of the total cost within the first two years. Moreover, there were capacity and safety gains, including new buses that would have had to be added in the coming years at additional costs, thereby maximizing the initial savings. The total savings amounted to hundreds of thousands of dollars that were reallocated to meet new demands. Thus, these contracts can be viewed as a viable source of mining for newfound dollars. Administrators should review all contracts with vendors, especially at the time of renewal, for possible cost savings.

So far we have been talking about the various line items within the budget but not about entire programs. Franzi argues, however, that we *should* be looking at each program from year to year to identify those that are no longer working or adding value to the organization and thus could be discontinued to free up funds for new activities that *will* add value, such as technology. Although this idea will likely be controversial, it is critical to the achievement of the school's core mission—providing the best possible program for its students. Franzi's point is that what worked last year may not work today and may be completely inadequate for tomorrow as needs and conditions change. While we are fond of thinking about the change process with respect to district programs, we are not accustomed to applying that same reasoning to the budget process.

Finally, there is the ever-important *control* element of the budgeting process. Once we are into the new budget cycle, the goal is to manage spending according to the plan—which is an ongoing process. This is done by what Franzi refers to as monthly, rolling reforecasts of each budget line against the plan—looking for areas of potential trouble (deficit) as expenditures are projected to the end of the year. This requires sophisticated techniques that should be followed by all budget administrators and shared with school and department leaders.

Franzi suggests the following strategies among the set of reforecasting tools for building a yearly reforecast for any school district.

- Review previous years' spending patterns and rates of spending for all accounts.
- Identify any historical aberrations in spending that may have an impact in the year being forecast.
- Identify any unplanned expenditure from prior periods that may reoccur in the current year.
- Review any accounts affected by seasonality (e.g., utilities).
- Review personnel accounts for changes in staff, retirees, and new hires with a lower or higher cost base than originally planned.
- Identify changes in enrollment that may have an impact on spending in instructional accounts.
- Conduct a thorough review of expense areas such as health insurance (if self-funded). These accounts tend to be oversensitive to timing and amount of individual claims. Consult your provider, if necessary, to develop a solid plan for the balance of the year.
- Review all other accounts for under/overspending against original budget plan.
- Discuss any changes in the program that may impact spending in the months ahead.
- Conduct an extensive special education analysis in the areas of outplacement and settlements; frequent meetings should occur between

the special education administration and the business office to prevent surprises.

- Review the substance and timing of any in-kind services from the township/municipality (such as athletic field maintenance).
- Manage any contractual renewals with service providers to enhance savings and/or cost avoidance for subsequent periods.
- Perform reforecasts tied to payroll and payable periods on a frequent basis.

Thus, the reforecast process is an information management technique for decision-making in the running of district financial operations. It requires frequent dialogue among administration to (1) identify any needed corrective measures throughout the year and (2) manage issues before they become large problems. Moreover, if done frequently, it fine-tunes the true spending levels of the district's accounts and assists in the budget development process for the following cycle. By using these techniques, major deficits can be identified early and dealt with successfully, as the case study discussed later in this chapter will show.

The Role of School and Department Leaders

Principals and department leaders play an important role throughout this process as they (1) communicate needs and priorities and (2) work with faculty and staff to build consensus. Building and department administrators must, therefore, be engaged in these processes to fully understand the scope of their operations. Resource control and allocation are important leadership issues for organizational success. Through in-depth involvement in the process, administrators will be better able to communicate the need for ongoing changes to faculty and staff when unforeseen and unplanned events, such as enrollment increases or large, unexpected increases in medical care costs, put upward pressure on their operational budgets.

Franzi notes that all administrators must have an innate capacity to anticipate unplanned events to know where there is flexibility in their budgets to be able to absorb these events and hold to the original spending plan. Without in-depth experience with these processes, unplanned events may impact program or instructional budgets to the extent that the rate of planned spending in those programs must be curtailed. Principals and department leaders need to know and understand these forces to be able to react to and properly communicate changing needs and priorities to their staff. For example, when health care costs soar, which is not a budget line item that principals and department leaders generally work with, they must be able to explain the reasons for the upward pressure and why there is an impact on supply budgets. The following case study will bring all of these issues together.

Case Study: Impact of Health Care Costs on District Spending

This is a real case study of a problem encountered by a New England school district for which Franzi was called in to help resolve and establish effective budgeting procedures.

Statement of the Problem

As of January, midway through the budget year, Mr. Lake, the district's budget director, determined that the medical claims budget was 91 percent expended. Based on monthly expenditures projected to the end of the budget year, he determined that the budget shortfall could be as high as 2 percent of the total operating budget. Because it was midway through the budget year, fully making up 2 percent of the total operating budget over only a six-month time period was equivalent to a 4 percent budget impact. Lake's task was to persuade policy makers to deal with the problem in ways that (1) did not end in a budget deficit, (2) had minimal impact on instruction, and (3) established a change in district and town policy to ensure that this problem would not reoccur.

Background/Context of the Problem

The town had been absorbing part of the district's insurance costs within its budget for years. Hence the board of education had, in effect, not been setting aside appropriate funds to cover its claims expenses for health insurance. In this particular case, both the town and the board of education were in a combined, self-insured, health care plan. This approach to paying for health care costs is generally accepted as smart budgeting for municipalities and schools. The problem was that they did not have an aggregate "stop loss" provision that would kick in at a predetermined rate of overspending. This is an expensive provision in the health care contract and, since major medical expenses had not been a problem for this district in the past, it was not seen as necessary. But recent high-cost medical problems for several staff were now putting severe upward pressure on this account. As a result, incurred costs on claims now presented a challenge to the board of education in terms of planning for the appropriate level of budget funds to cover expenses.

Analysis of the Problem

Claims expenses and their projection are typically managed by the insurance provider through trend analyses and actual experience. The issue the board of education faced was how proactive the insurance provider had been in managing this information to prevent cost overruns. Consequently, if the provider was not proactive (the problem in this case), unplanned expenses would be incurred, thereby impacting the board's budget in any given year. Additionally, there are several other factors that could impact spending levels in this account, such as an aging population (faculty and staff), lack of an aggregate stop loss provision in the health care contract with the provider, and supplemental assessments by the insurance provider. All of these issues were now impacting this board's budget.

Actions Taken

Once the problem was identified and understood, what actions did the budget director and board of education need to take?

The most immediate challenge was to develop a tactical plan to deal with the cost overruns, which were impacting all areas of the budget. Their plan was to freeze the budget midway through the year and have principals and department leaders assess their planned expenses for the balance of the year. They would then provide Mr. Lake with input as to where they could (1) slow the rate of spending or (2) completely curtail spending in an area of the budget. The principals' leadership roles were critically important in this process, as only they could assess the instructional impact of any changes and prioritize actions. Hence, their leadership roles were to understand the nature of the problem, determine priorities, and then communicate the need for change to their faculty, staff, and constituents (parents and students where appropriate). As these spending freezes and slow downs were implemented, the district used Franzi's rolling reforecasting techniques to provide ongoing current information on how well it was meeting its new budget plan.

Of course, a simple approach to resolving the problem would have been to go back to the town financing authority and ask for a mid-year special allocation. Franzi counseled the district out of this direction by arguing that a key function of any administration is to manage its finances. Doing so builds confidence in the administration and helps ensure that, when resources are truly needed, they are more likely to be allocated. For the long-term political stability of this district, Franzi advocated full disclosure with a short- and long-term plan to deal with the problem.

Thus, a long-term strategy had to be developed to ensure that this problem did not reoccur. In this case, the town and board of education pursued obtaining consulting services for the review of their existing health care plan, claims expenses incurred, and a proposal for options to control expenses. The board (and town) also adopted an individual stop loss provision for the upcoming budget year. Finally, the board considered modifying its negotiation strategy with all bargaining units to seek the right to engage other carriers for health insurance coverage, maintaining similar benefits for the plan participants, but one that would provide the board options to negotiate better rates with the insurance providers.

Outcome from the Actions Taken
Using these short-term tactics, the district had accumulated enough savings over the subsequent six-month period to cover the increases in the claims expense account and balance the budget by the end of the fiscal year. The key to success was early identification of an unplanned event (the problem was fully understood by mid-year) and then communication of that problem to the appropriate board(s). Subsequently, by having budgetary control processes in place, the district was able to make the decision to freeze or slow spending with some confidence that the large shortfall could be made up in a relatively short period of time. The problem was identified and controlled by establishing budget baselines and using rolling projections by line item. Since the total amount to be made up amounted to a net 4 percent of the operating budget, it was subsequently determined that some of the savings accrued could be reallocated to new priorities the following year. Thus, the district reallocated approximately 1.5 percent of the budget, which was enough to significantly add funds to the technology and staff development budgets. Most importantly, the administration maintained and increased its credibility with the board of education and the town finance board, making subsequent budget requests easier to secure.

Summary

Budgetary control and reallocation are excellent examples of data-driven decision-making. Moreover, they are critical functions necessary for effectively developing and managing the budget in ways that help the district achieve its mission. Franzi argues that the purpose of a budget is to achieve the organization's goals. As we will see in the next chapter on organizational effectiveness, the only constant in today's educational environment is change. Thus, changing conditions and priorities place constant pressure on budgets that need to be more dynamic and flexible to meet current needs. Using budgetary control and reallocation methodologies discussed in this chapter will provide some measure of control on spending and allow districts to modify their budget plans to meet new and competing demands for resources.

CHAPTER SIX

~

Achieving School Improvement through Data-Driven Decision-Making and Systems Thinking

Change is now occurring at rates thought unimaginable only decades ago. The speed of change is a geometric progression with knowledge doubling every ten years or less. A colleague puts it this way: "In the past, today and tomorrow were like yesterday, but in the twenty-first century, today is different than yesterday, and tomorrow can't be predicted."[1] In a little over one hundred years, we have transformed from an agricultural through an industrial to a knowledge economy. And information technologies may now be transforming the economy again into something as yet undefined. In the recent past, change was episodic; that is, when change occurred, it was toward a destination such as a modification to the reading program. Once that change was made, staff felt it was time to look at another program area, satisfied that the reading change would last for some time. But today, change is more a process or a journey without any particular destination. Changing demographics and needs of students, staff members retiring or moving, changes in leadership, funding fluctuations—all contribute to the continuous need for a flexible, ever-changing organization. And while we can agree that school improvement occurs when interventions are made that are well thought out, properly implemented, and based upon analyses of current versus desired performance, getting a handle on just what the "current state is" is becoming more and more difficult due to our constantly changing organizations. As for figuring out what the "desired" state is, Senge et al.[2] note that "The safest prediction is change; schools can no longer prepare people to fit in the world of twenty years ago, because that world will no longer exist." Thus, the purpose of this chapter is to describe how improvement initiatives, to be most effective, must be woven into the fabric of the organization using systems thinking.

Why systems thinking? We know, for example, that effective principals make a real difference, but so does a curriculum aligned to challenging standards. In many school settings, rigorous testing programs have become a catalyst for improvement; yet, testing alone without proper preparation and follow-up can turn into a destructive influence. We are led to believe that the suburbs do the best job; however, there are many examples of urban schools' excelling, as noted in a report released by the U.S. Department of Education (http://www.ed.gov/pubs/urbanhope/). Further, almost no one would suggest that what works in the suburbs will work in the cities, as the organizational cultures and problems are so different. Thus, it seems as though addressing the issue of school improvement as we have in the past, as a destination rather than a continuous journey without paying attention to the interrelatedness of interventions, existing programs, and systems, is a little like trying to stem the leak in the dam: when you plug one hole, another almost immediately opens up.

Achieving a high level of effectiveness for complex organizations requires systems integration. Thus, when we decide to run a pilot program or implement a particular intervention, we will want to be sure that all necessary activities are interrelated. This can be difficult in educational settings as, for example, curriculum departments do not often get involved with the hiring of new staff. Conversely, principals, who typically do the hiring, are not often curriculum or content specialists. How, then, can we ensure the integration of ideas and actions? And as school and district organizations become larger, there exist even fewer connections among the departments and schools, let alone between the senior leadership team members who develop plans and those tasked with carrying them out—teachers and principals. All of this organizational complexity points to the need for systems thinking and action. Tom Peters,[3] the organizational guru of the 1990s, warns that hierarchical organizations (which characterize many schools) are inefficient, making it even more important to employ a systems thinking approach to organizational effectiveness.

Third-Generation Systems Thinking

Third-generation systems thinking is an emerging field of practice that may hold some promise for success in education. As noted by many on the topic of systems thinking, the field has transformed itself over the years through three iterations, or generations, of thinking.[4-8] Early first-generation systems thinking "dealt with the challenge of interdependency in the context of mechanical (deterministic) systems."[9] In contrast, effective organizations today are made up of anything but mechanical—deterministic—systems. Everything is dynamic, forever changing as global economies and politics impact almost every decision that is made.[10-16] In dealing with this dynamic environment, systems thinking changed, too, to deal with "the dual challenges of interdependency and self-organization (neg-entropy) in the context of living systems."[17] However, this second-generation systems thinking of cybernetics and "open systems" failed to take into account the "sociocultural" context of systems. As Gharajedaghi explains, old thinking held that outcomes were a factor of a set of independent variables acting in some linear fashion, as noted in Figure 6.1.

Applying the problem of school improvement to this formula, we would be led to believe that improvement is a linear function of the various systems under our control. This approach assumes that these variables are simply independent—not also highly interdependent. This approach was abandoned by most private-sector organizations because it failed to take into account the interrelatedness of these independent variables in a socially complex environment. Clearly, our experience tells us that it does not work in schools either.

Linear Systems Thinking

$$Y = fF (x1, x2, x3, x4)$$

$$Y \text{ (Dependent)} = F \text{ (Independent Variables)}$$

$$S\text{chool } I\text{mprovement} = PE, P, M\&L, PD\&E$$

PE=Program Evaluation
P = Planning
M&L = Management and Leadership
PD&E = Professional Development and Evaluation

Figure 6.1   Adaptation of Linear Systems Thinking to School Improvement

Third-generation systems thinking "responds to the triple challenges of interdependency, self-organization, and choice in the context of sociocultural systems."[18] Such a shift in thinking requires an effort to meet constantly changing conditions and problems. These conditions require "a shift in our assumptions regarding the method of inquiry, the means of knowing, from analytical thinking (the science of dealing with independent sets of variables) to holistic thinking (the art and science of handling interdependent sets of variables)."[19] Wheatley[20] also argues for a new way of dealing with organizational problems and uncertainty, basing her approach on the science of quantum mechanics where change is a constant, nothing is as it appears, and action taken on one variable *always* affects other variables—often in unexpected ways. Gharajedaghi refers to this variation in thinking as a paradigm shift from an analytical approach to a systems approach applied through a "multi-minded system" or social model of organizational structure. Gharajedaghi displays this new way of thinking, or third-generation systems thinking, in Figure 6.2. Here, each variable is both independent (i.e., choices are made within each system or function) and interdependent, as the actions taken in one system affect the actions and outcomes in every other system.

Third-Generation Systems Thinking:
Interdependency and Choice within Systems

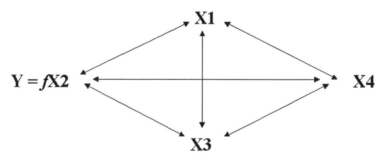

Figure 6.2 Gharajedaghi: Third-Generation Systems Thinking

Applying Systems Thinking

Peters[21] brings these ideas together nicely, especially as they apply to larger school organizations:

Fact is . . . [that] systems are (far) more important than ever before. We are routinely accomplishing large projects . . . working with hundreds of people . . . from hither and thither . . . many (most?) of whom we've never met.

The ethereal organization/disembodied organization/disintermediated organization/transparent organization . . . demands great systems. And therein lies the rub. Most of our systems are jury-rigged, bogged down in detail (even post-reengineering). So we need some new ways of thinking about systems.

Peters reminds us that organizational success requires that we get smarter about systems' self-importance and interrelatedness. Applying multidimensional systems thinking to schools (Figure 6.3), Gharajedaghi's model begins to describe what needs to take place for meaningful school improvement.

Schools are highly social organizations in which culture is an important factor and can have a major impact on operations and effectiveness. Sergiovanni[22] discusses the interplay between systems and culture, or the "life-world" of leadership, arguing that the "system's world"—"a world of instrumentalities usually experienced in schools as management systems"—should be driven by the life-world comprised of "culture, meaning, and significance"—not the other way around. As in most complex organizations, the

Third-Generation Systems Thinking
Interdependency and Choice within Systems—Modified for Education

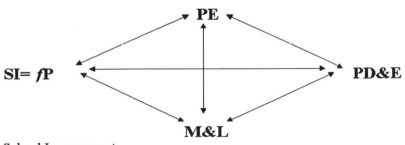

SI = School Improvement
P = Planning
PE = Program Evaluation
M&L = Management and Leadership
PD&E = Professional Development and Evaluation

Figure 6.3 Adaptation of Third-Generation Systems Thinking to School Improvement

systems I discuss here (planning, program evaluation, organizational management, resources and leadership, professional development, and evaluation) are by themselves independent of one another. As independent systems, they make choices—about what problems are addressed, what steps are followed, which changes are made—that affect, directly or indirectly, each of the other systems. It is generally agreed that this model of system *independency* using primarily analytical procedures has led to organizational ineffectiveness in almost every sector of society as problems and issues have become more and more complex and socially interconnected.[23-30] To the extent that this "out-dated" organizational structure describes school settings, a change in approach is needed. However, from a purely practical point of view, it will not be possible for schools to change their organizational structures overnight, but it may be possible to change organizational *practice* with respect to school improvement activities. And it would seem appropriate to adopt a third-generation systems model for that shift in practice, given the complex nature of school improvement problems—keeping in mind that these systems must be guided by the "life-world" of the organization. Thus, what follows is a description of an "integrated systems approach" to school improvement to help achieve that goal, with a full discussion of the leadership implications to ensure that systems do not drive culture.

What Are the Educational Systems That We Can Most Control?

The systems over which we have most control are (1) program evaluation and development, (2) planning, (3) organizational management (including fiscal and human resources, and leadership), and (4) professional development and evaluation. Functions such as policy development and political management are included within the management and leadership frame.

The literature is robust for each of these systems, thus my purpose is to not review that literature supporting the need for or to defend the importance of these systems. Rather, it is to explore how these systems become interrelated and interdependent in a third-generation systems thinking approach that leads to a broader understanding of how schools can operate more flexibly and dynamically to achieve meaningful improvement. In fact, one can make an argument that the school improvement process needs to be *both* analytical and holistic. It is analytical insofar as, once the leadership team decides to embark on an improvement project, there is a definite sequence of activities to follow. Yet it is also holistic in that what we learn from dealing with organizational changes may have an impact on some of the earlier decisions made, such as strategic plans and resource allocation decisions. For example, what is learned from one set of actions designed to improve writing instruction could easily affect the language arts curriculum and its delivery or organizational structure. Thus, one improvement process can often affect another. Most importantly, all of this activity is carried out in living, breathing, changing, socially dynamic organizations where the only constant is change itself.

Operationalizing an Integrated Systems Approach to School Improvement

Choosing the phrase "operationalizing an *integrated systems* approach to school improvement" is redundant because a systems approach necessitates system integration. However, I have used the phrase to emphasize the importance of holistic thinking in this process. For a complete review of the application of systems thinking to these problems, a thorough review of third-generation systems thinking can be found among several texts. Gaynor's *Analyzing Problems in Schools and School Systems*[31] takes a theoretical approach to understanding school problems, exploring several systems, such as school political and social systems. Gaynor uses systems thinking as a way to build models for decision-making by using feedback systems. These models are referred to as archetypes by Senge[32] and referred to as mental models discussed by O'Connor and McDermott.[33] Gharajedaghi's[34] *Systems Thinking: Managing Chaos and Complexity* presents a highly useful explanation of systems thinking for improving organizations—the subject of much of this chapter. *The Art of Systems Thinking: Essential Skills for Creativity and Problem Solving*[35] discusses approaches to systems thinking, what the authors term "thinking in circles," and the need for feedback loops, which, as we see, is a critical component of a systems approach stressed so heavily by Senge.

O'Connor and McDermott also introduce the concept of mental models and their importance in solving problems. Senge et al.,[36] in *The Fifth Discipline Fieldbook: Strategies and Tools for Building a Learning Organization*, use the concept of archetypes to describe these mental models or approaches to problem solving, offering several examples. Senge and colleagues'[37,38] view of systems thinking and its importance for organizational success provides the conceptual framework for the practices discussed in this book. Senge and others have extended this thinking to the public sector in *The Dance of Change: The Challenges to Sustaining Momentum in Learning Organizations*,[39] and specifically to school in *Schools That Learn: A Fifth Discipline Fieldbook for Educators*,

Parents, and Everyone Who Cares about Education.[40] Finally, Scott's *Organizations: Rational, Natural, and Open Systems*[41] presents a thorough application of systems thinking as it relates to every aspect of organizational effectiveness. Taken together, these works provide the foundation and rationale for looking at school improvement holistically, not analytically—and dynamically, not statically. Moreover, since all of this activity takes place *in* schools, which are among the most socially complex organizations within society, a model is needed that can respond quickly to socially complex dynamics. Bolman and Deal[42] and Sergiovanni[43] address these issues of systems integration and inter-relatedness while maintaining a broader focus on effective leadership, organizational culture, and effectiveness.

Integrating the Systems

The interplay in and among these systems is shown in Figure 6.4. Here, the major systems are shown with their high level of "integratedness." At the top of the model, goals and objectives are developed through a constant give-and-take between program evaluation activities, review of standards, and planning for change to (1) meet higher levels of achievement, (2) make

An Integrated Systems Approach to School Improvement

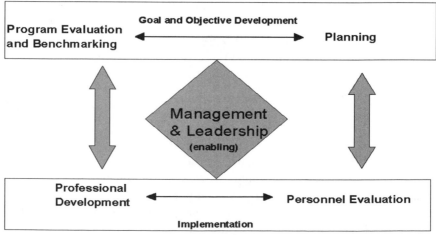

Figure 6.4   Systems Thinking Applied to School Improvement

needed changes, and/or (3) set new improvement targets or benchmarks. While school leaders act to enable the goal- and objective-setting practices through effective leadership and managerial practice, they do not implement those changes without help. Teachers, principals, and parents make substantive changes at the school level and are aided in their work by effective professional development programs. Professional staff are then held accountable through personnel evaluation practices.

Within this systems approach, various related activities can be occurring at once, hence, a holistic approach. For example, if a district has concluded an evaluation of its middle school writing program and established plans for improvement to change how writing instruction is delivered and by whom (i.e., should it be a separate writing teacher or the student's language arts teacher?), it might find that, in altering the organizational structure to have writing delivered by the language arts teachers, two things happen. First, there will be a need for professional development for the language arts teachers to implement these changes and, second, there might be a significant impact on the language arts program staffing, and indeed the structure of the school, such as the organization of teams at the middle school level. In fact, making this change in writing instruction could negatively affect the social development goal of the middle school if the structure of the teaming organizations is dramatically affected. Thus, systems thinking is necessary to take into account all the possibilities and to sort out all of this change. In the final analysis, making the needed improvement in writing instruction might be implemented with less impact on the total organization by restructuring the staffing model to include a writing expert on each team to serve as a mentor to the other teachers. As a result of these modifications, the dynamics of integrated instruction could change across the other subjects as well, since writing across the curriculum is an important schoolwide function. In the end, both writing and language arts instruction could be improved with little or no additional staffing costs.

So, in summary, what might start out as a straightforward writing project could easily turn out to have a significant impact on organizational structure and staffing across many subject areas. This story is a true recounting of how one suburban school district addressed its writing problem. As one administrator later recounted, "Who would have thought that a simple look at writing instruction would turn out to be so complicated?" But, in applying systems thinking, this district successfully addressed all of the related issues and dynamics needed for success. This district's writing *and* language arts achievement greatly improved over the next three years.

Both "Integrated" and "Sequential" Systems

To be truly effective, data analysis should be conducted within a school improvement context and for an expressed purpose. The contexts in which we conduct these analyses are the major systems over which we have control. As noted earlier, these systems include:

1. Program evaluation
2. Planning
3. Management and leadership
4. Personnel evaluation and professional development

For school improvement purposes, these systems should be thought of as both integrated and sequential. They are integrated in that they are part of a larger school "system" in which various component parts are constantly interacting with each other. Yet as we look at a particular problem, the systems need to be carried out in a logical sequence. Lets take the previously discussed writing instruction problem to another level.

As the New Heights Middle School evaluates its various programs through a combination of state mastery tests and its own internal assessment tools, it finds that students in eighth grade are not writing as well as expected. Thus, the processes that follow will be critical to the overall improvement of student writing. The first step is to marshal resources, both human and financial, to address the achievement problem. This necessitates a planning process at the district level through which school leaders and board members decide to allocate time and resources to the improvement of student writing over other programs that might also need attention. From all of this activity, someone on the senior leadership team needs to decide where limited resources will be allocated. This is clearly a planning and prioritization function. Following a decision to focus resources on improving writing, attention needs to be paid to the leadership and organizational/management structure needed to bring about the desired change. For example, the school might need to make organizational/management changes in how writing instruction is scheduled. It may also determine that it lacks the expertise at the program level to guide this change, requiring the hiring of a writing expert, either as a consultant or in some formal leadership role within the school (or district). There would also be the need to explain to the faculty and administration why these changes are needed. In doing so, the senior district leadership team would want to lay out a plan that engages faculty and building administrators in the process of understanding why the changes are needed and in designing and implementing solutions/changes. Once the solutions have been identified, there will be a need to train teachers on new approaches to the teaching of writing through the professional development program, and then to hold them accountable, over time, for implementing those changes through the personnel evaluation system.

The overall process described here is sequential, insofar as program evaluation and benchmarking against external standards provide the basis that enables educators to prioritize and focus resources through the planning process. In the planning process, competing needs are prioritized to maximize the impact of limited district resources. Once this process has been completed and the district initiatives have been selected, school leadership, management, and organizational structures need to be reviewed to ensure that they are aligned to meet the strategic goals and objectives of the district. Also, a need emerges at this stage to fully engage those most affected by the decision—teachers—in understanding the need for change and in helping to design potential solutions. As teachers and school administrators begin to implement these solutions, they should be trained and then held accountable over time for carrying out those changes that have been agreed to.

In the final analysis it will be the teaching staff that is called upon to make program modifications. We should rely on their vast experience by providing them the relevant data and asking them to consider their implications for change. With teachers' buy-in to the need for change, coupled with their "in the trenches" expertise, improvement is all but assured.

The Bigger Picture

The sequence of activities for each development project is determined by a logical set of processes and procedures that are necessary to bring about educational change. Since planning for change needs to be designed from an analysis of current performance in relation to both internal and external standards, we should logically begin with some process of program evaluation. *And it is here that data-driven decision-making is practiced/applied.* This can take the form of an internal district/school review of its achievement indices or a comparison of those indices to some external standard as discussed in earlier chapters. In so doing, benchmarks for improvement are identified.

Next, these evaluation outcomes and findings must be considered within the overall context of the school organization. Here, competing demands are prioritized within the planning process and resources are allocated among these competing demands. Once a "go" decision is made in the planning function, leadership must embrace the change, explain its rationale to those who will implement the change, and modify the organizational structures to meet these new conditions. Professional development, as needed, also needs to be provided to assist those who will carry out the change.

Finally, those responsible within the organization for implementing change should be held accountable through the evaluation process over a reasonable period of time. Barring too many distractions or "bumps in the road," this process should take about three years to complete and take hold in most school settings. Ironically, it is these very distractions and bumps in the road that force us to think systemically as we consider needed modifications to our "plan" along the way, asking how these changes will affect other operations. The result of this holistic review is likely to result in positive influences on the change process; hence, it should be considered a valuable distraction that can keep us from making organizational blunders. This process or sequence is shown in Figure 6.5.

Finally, there is an interplay or interrelatedness between the various on-going activities, as discussed earlier. Employing systems thinking requires that we constantly be aware that the impact of changes made in X not only affect Y, but also many other variables as well, and often, in unexpected ways. This view is represented in Figure 6.6.

A Systems Approach to School Improvement

Figure 6.5   Systems Thinking Applied to School Improvement

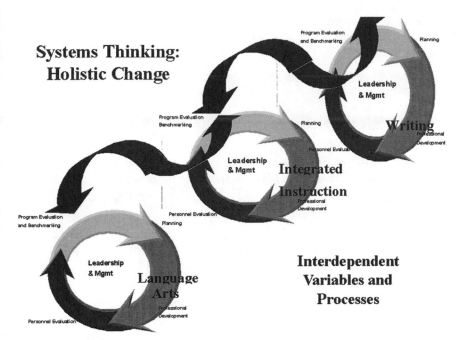

Systems Thinking: Holistic Change

Interdependent Variables and Processes

Figure 6.6   Systems Thinking and Interdependency

A Helicopter View

To manage and lead schools within this expanded context requires not only holistic systems thinking, it also requires a "helicopter view" of the organization. A colleague, Charles Mojkowski, and I explored this problem a few years back and coined the phrase "helicopter view" as a result of our beliefs on how school leaders must change their thinking.[44] By this we mean the ability to synthesize the multitude of information flowing within the organization, to step above the detail, to make sense of the chaos, and turn that stream of data into meaningful information for decision-making. Third-generation systems thinking is an appropriate operational model to use in this context because it enables one to manage the chaos and complexity of modern organizations from a more global perspective or vantage point.[45]

Data-Driven Decision-Making and Fast-Track Evaluation

Within this context, program evaluation is the key starting point for improvement. To quote an old phrase, "It's hard to know where you're going without knowing where you're at." In other words, you cannot know what to change unless you know current levels of organizational performance measured against some standard. And data-driven decision-making is a set of tools and processes for conducting program evaluation and monitoring ongoing program development.

When using these processes, four categories or frames of analyses can be conducted. But a first consideration is the level of sophistication of these analyses, which is highly dependent on two factors:

1. The quality of the data needed to address the problem, (i.e., is it appropriate to the analysis? Is it in the right measurement scale? Is there enough data over enough cohorts to render the analysis meaningful?)
2. Is that data readily accessible for analysis?

Experience tells us that districts typically do have high-quality data to address their mission critical goals and objectives, but that these data are not easily accessible. This problem will be the subject of chapter 8, in which the use of data warehouses, information technologies, and decision-support tools are discussed for conducting fast-track evaluation. Once the quality, quantity, and accessibility of data are reviewed, we can move to the actual analyses. As discussed throughout the earlier chapters of this book, four major categories of evaluation can be used to drive improvement.

Four Frames (Categories) for Evaluation

A popular analysis/activity is the disaggregation of data for equity analyses[46,47] (see chapter 3). Here, school leaders disaggregate data by gender, race, ethnic background, socioeconomic status, and various cohort groups (e.g., special program participation) to determine if student outcome variables differ according to these designations. The school goal is to attain equitable student performance across these variables. And through data disaggregation and appropriate statistical analyses, we can often determine if improvement strategies are needed for a special population. A second category, and one that is much more difficult to accomplish due to the frequent inaccessibility of data, is the analysis of specific student cohorts over time or the longitudinal analysis of student performance data (see chapter 2). Through this process we can evaluate performance against benchmarks and then set improvement targets based on organizational performance over time. We can also establish reasonable and attainable improvement targets for students and schools. While this is arguably one of the more important categories of program evaluation, as it focuses on the overall improvement of everyone within the organization, it is also one of the more difficult to conduct because of the technical problems of bringing all of the data together in one database for proper analysis.

The third category is one that I have termed "exploring" (see chapter 4), and it encompasses the analysis of a particular grade or group of students to determine if improvement is needed, having no apparent indication that there is a problem. For example, a school might want to try to identify evidence of grade inflation in a particular course, group of courses, subject area, or group of teachers. Or they might want to know what the impact is of students' outside work after hours or the impact of student participation in sports and cocurricular activities on the overall achievement of those students.

A colleague recently wanted to know if the change in algebra programming across two years had a positive effect on student grades, expressed as more As and Bs and fewer Ds and Fs. Through an exploring session with his data warehouse, we were able to develop the proper query and extract the results (the new program was indeed working!). Finally, one could argue that data disaggregation for equity analyses is a form of exploring, but it has been separated in this book to give it special attention due to the scope of the national interest in the equity agenda. That agenda is important, but more focused than exploring. We can think of exploring as analogous to MBWA—management by wandering around—only, in exploring, we are using data and analyses as the vehicle for "wandering around." My colleague thought of the question as we were discussing math programs, thus, we went on an exploration to discover the status of the new program.

The final category has to do with cost control and budgetary allocation for the purposes of understanding the limits of the financial resources in the district, school, or program—so as to better maximize use of the finances for the successful attainment of our goals (see chapter 5). A differentiation is made here between cost-benefit analyses and the review of costs as they relate to program effectiveness. Cost-benefit analyses, such as those typically used in business and industry, are highly specialized activities that do not readily apply to school organizations. However, that does not mean that we should ignore these procedures and relationships altogether. Our work on data-driven decision-making tells us that there are imprecise but usable ways to review the relationship between costs and effectiveness.

The real problem here is that we have imprecise dependent variables, and we have statistical difficulty linking independent variables in a causal manner—needed for cost-benefit analyses. For example, one Connecticut school district was interested in learning if their special elementary reading and math "pull-out" enrichment program was having a positive effect on achievement. The district had collected the "correct" data to isolate students in the program and to measure fall to spring growth of several cohorts over several elementary schools. The analysis we did indicated that the fall to spring growth in every classroom was positive and significant. That analysis was used to prove, from a cost-benefit point of view, that the program should be retained. But, as a researcher, I could cite numerous "threats" to the validity and reliability of the measures and techniques used in this cost-benefit analysis. For example, we would have to ask to what extent the measures used actually measure what was intended and/or taught. What other factors could have contributed to the results—such as the regular education program—and so on? But for this colleague, the results were persuasive enough within a fast-track data-driven decision-making framework. And they were persuasive for me, too; if I were superintendent I would have run with it also. As our data collection strategies improve along with the tools needed for analysis, these inquiries may approach traditional, private-sector, cost-benefit analysis precision. But for now, most schools do not have this level of expertise and will have to limit those discussions to two areas of financial inquiry: cost control and budgetary allocation.

These, then, are areas of inquiry that principals, program directors, and data teams can use to maximize limited resources and improvement. These four areas of program evaluation are shown in Figure 6.7.

Data-Driven Decision-Making: Four Frames Program Evaluation Analyses

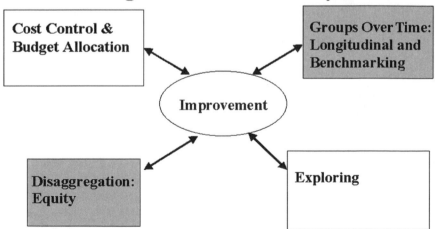

Figure 6.7   Data-Driven Decision-Making: Frames of Analysis

Fast-Track Evaluation: What Is It and Why Do It?

Decisions and actions dominate our fast-paced world. Almost everywhere we look, major decisions are made quickly because the analyses that support these decisions are typically conducted in short time frames to meet the demands of accountability and the value of our time that drive our society. From corporate mergers to individual investors' analyses of stocks, these analyses are performed quickly and easily using information technologies and new, on-line decision-support tools. Even the purchase of a home or automobile is now made more convenient by using these tools. Web-based real estate services provide buyers the ability to search properties via the Internet by price range, community, and housing type, thereby maximizing their available time for on-site home inspection. The same holds true for car buyers, but here, the consumer can avoid entering the showroom by shopping and ordering on-line—conducting all the research and the entire transaction in cyber space. Internet-based sales of just about everything—from airline tickets to exotic collectibles—can be now accessed from our living rooms— or even while mobile (many digital cell phones now enable you to log onto the Internet). Various on-line trading services allow us to buy and sell literally anything on-line. Compared to what existed only a few years ago as "past practice" for all of these examples, one could call current practice a form of fast-track analysis and decision-making.

But this transformation has not spread to the world of public education. Local educators are typically left to evaluating programs using methods that are extremely labor-intensive, requiring the gathering of disparate data (sometimes having to re-key that data into some form of electronic spreadsheet or database for processing and then move that database into an analysis program to run statistics). All of this takes too much time and energy and too many resources. Worse, decision-makers do not often have the proper data to fit traditional research questions, so plans have to be put in place to administer surveys, conduct observations, or administer new tests to gather the data needed to match the needs of the program evaluation questions. This process, which can take up to eighteen months to complete, no longer meets the needs of schools. What is needed is an evaluation process that can be implemented locally that relies on existing (legacy) data and retains the most important components of standard evaluation methods and is more dynamic, flexible, and capable of completion in hours, days, or weeks—not months or years. Just as the prospective homeowner no longer has the time to visit hundreds of homes, busy school leaders no longer have the luxury nor time to review, gather, collate, transform, and analyze the mounds of data regularly collected in their schools. We need a more efficient way of conducting these analyses at the local level.

Further complicating this problem is the fact that standard program evaluation methods may be subject to serious limitations concerning the utility of their findings. These methods often require twelve to eighteen months of analysis and review before action can be taken. Schools are dynamic organizations, and a great deal of change can take place over that time period. Moreover, traditional approaches to program evaluation do not typically take into consideration existing conditions due to resource limitations. (By existing conditions, I mean "real-time" conditions that exist at the time the report is reviewed for decision-making. In the traditional process of program review, data are collected and analyzed and a report is prepared. Typically this process can take a year or more. But when the final report is issued, "real-time" current conditions in the school are not accounted for. In-out migration, for example, could have seriously changed the make-up of the student body during this time lag. Staff resignations and retirements, too, can impact real-time conditions. Decision-making today requires a review of past performance but must take into account current conditions to the greatest extent possible.) Because of the complexity of data acquisition and analysis used in traditional approaches, consideration of existing conditions would throw the time frame off by another six to twelve months, costing additional resources. In fact, we would be in a constant time lag, unable to catch-up to real-life conditions. Thus, this time lag not being captured through standard program evaluation practices presents serious limitations for schools as they struggle with a highly complex and dynamically changing environment. The problem is not with the research methods, but with the access to relevant, up-to-date data. Thus, a method of real-time data analyses and ongoing evaluation is needed.

Finally, just as the purchase of a home requires some risk taking in making a "buy decision" (based on an assumption of current market conditions), school leadership requires a certain level of risk taking to make decisions based on available data. However, that risk should still be data-driven as much as possible, just as is the purchase of a home. The trick here is to know or "sense" when the gathering and analysis of additional data has the potential to seriously and negatively impact the decision-making process. For example, we might risk making a lower offer by perhaps $10,000 on a home with a $150,000 asking price knowing that this offer will still be "in the ball park" as a result of our ongoing data analysis of market conditions and mortgage interest rates. At one point, though, we need to make a decision to make an offer (do we offer $140,000 or $150,000?) in consideration of changing market conditions and interest rates that could render that $10,000 savings meaningless over the course of a thirty-year mortgage that is rising one-third of a point per month. At this point continual data gathering can become unproductive. With schools, we often reach this point when we require additional data that won't be available for months or even years (for example, surveys of parent and community attitudes and additional student testing data not yet in place). In these cases we need to ask ourselves if holding off action to conduct these analyses will be worthwhile in the long run and what the costs of inaction might be.

While schools regularly collect data, there is virtually no way to access these data quickly for "on the fly" decisions that need to be made, insofar as schools are managed day by day and hour by hour. The consequence of this problem is that decisions school leaders make that affect students', parents', and teachers' lives must be based on what I have come to term "informed intuition." Informed by the literature, school leaders have a good sense about the relationship between these variables, but they have almost no real way of knowing to what extent those findings hold true in their local school or district. *What is needed is a system for fast-track analysis and evaluation, along with a method of extracting the needed data quickly and easily.*

Fast-track evaluation can be described as the analysis of existing school data for improvement purposes, retaining the key elements and safeguards of traditional program evaluation but conducting the entire process through information technologies to speed the process. While fast-track evaluation retains the critical components of traditional evaluation, it can be conducted much more quickly and inexpensively.

Standard approaches to the analysis of data using paper reports, combined with the tedious process of gathering data and entering that data into a spreadsheet or small database, are, in-fact, examples of data-driven decision-making, but this process lacks dynamic flexibility. If the results are not made available for several months or more, critical factors may have changed over that time period. For example, many schools experience a 10 to 20 percent student turnover in a school year. If the results of the evaluation fail to account for this fundamental change in the nature of the student body, the overall results and their utility in planning for change must be questioned.

Data warehouses and new information technologies linked to powerful but easy-to-use decision-support tools (discussed in chapter 8) have the power to provide local educators the ability to conduct fast-track evaluation and data-driven decision-making. Using emerging information technologies such as data warehouses, educational decision-making can become more data-driven, thereby strengthening and supporting educators' intuition about what needs changing.

Enabled by these decision-support tools, what are the critical components of fast-track evaluation and data-driven decision-making? The primary processes that comprise data-driven decision-making are (1) understanding the problem and framing it into its logical components for analysis; (2) gathering the needed data; (3) conducting the analyses; (4) generating possible solutions; and (5) selecting a course of action to follow. Fast-track evaluation requires that we conduct an audit of existing data to determine if the problem(s) under review can, in fact, be answered with those data. If the data do not exist or are not accessible, then the question needs to be modified to fit that which can be asked within reasonable statistical limitations. Only as a last resort, when little or no useful data exist to answer the basic questions under review, should we consider dropping the question altogether. In cases where it is determined that the problem requires the collection of new data, a cost-benefit review of collecting that data should be conducted. If the cost-benefit analysis indicates that the answers gained through acquiring this data outweigh the costs of collection, both human and financial, then a "data acquisition plan" should be developed and implemented to collect the needed data.

Data-driven decision-making borrows practices from the program evaluation literature, paying attention to (1) which cohort groups are being analyzed and for what purposes, (2) determining what analyses should be conducted (making sure that these analyses are correct and appropriate to the questions under study), and (3) determining whether the available data is appropriate for the required analysis. It uses the benchmarking process to measure progress toward the attainment of some desired goal or standard. Data-driven decision-making and fast-track evaluation use data warehouses, information technologies, and decision-support tools to access and analyze data quickly and easily. These processes rely on the use of legacy data (defined here as the last and latest refresh of the data warehouse) to ensure that recent data are available to render the analyses relevant. With data warehouses, the data can be refreshed weekly, monthly, or quarterly, providing relevant and recent data upon which to make decisions. Inevitably, the decision as to what actions should be taken requires judgment and experience. Data-driven decision-making is not a substitute for wisdom, experience, and judgment. Rather, it supports decision-makers in their decision-making processes. There is also a danger of overreliance on statistical analyses. Decisions should neither be totally "data-based" nor should they be solely based on "informed intuition." The desired mix should be decisions that are predicated on experience and intuition informed by data. And no decision should be made without consulting those most affected—teachers. Using decision-support technologies, one can envision a group of teachers and administrators sitting around a table problem solving as they drill down into their data, gathering insights almost as quickly as they can generate the questions. The example sited earlier about the cost effectiveness of the special reading and math pull-out program emerged in just this setting. A Connecticut school district was training on its data warehouse, and the superintendent asked this very question. The group then developed a concept map of the problem, used the system to extract the needed data, ran the analyses, and reviewed the results. All of this took about half an hour.

Schools are every bit as complex and dynamic as major corporations with respect to their need to analyze data and make "mission-critical" decisions. By using information technologies and fast-track evaluation methods within a systems thinking framework, we can bring educational decision-making into the twenty-first century. We can also help our school leaders be more effective in their day-to-day management of schools and their strategic thinking and planning. By combining advancements in technology with the basics of program evaluation, fast-track evaluation and data-driven decision-making become attainable and can have a positive impact on the quality of decision-making.

Benchmarking as a Critical Function of Fast-Track Evaluation

Benchmarking is one of many tools used within a total quality management (TQM) framework for organizational improvement.[48,49] As applied to educational improvement, it is arguably the most important process of data-driven decision-making and, consequently, the fast-track evaluation processes. Benchmarking allows us to determine current levels of organizational performance and measure progress toward some goal over time. Without effective benchmarking to appropriate standards, the improvement process will likely fail.

It is important to note at this point that there is a difference between total quality management and systems thinking. As Gharajedaghi[50] puts it,

> There is a fundamental difference between TQM and systems thinking. TQM operates within an existing paradigm; it can be learned and applied as an independent set of tools and methods. But systems methodology cannot be separated from systems principles. Systems tools and methods are impotent if isolated from the paradigm of which they are an integral part.

There is a systems thinking methodology that entails reviewing and understanding the interrelatedness of function, structure, and purpose. These issues will be more fully described below, but in this section, emphasis will be placed on the importance of benchmarking for school improvement and to make the case that benchmarking as a TQM tool set and systems thinking, at least as it relates to school improvement, are not incompatible. In fact, they are absolutely essential processes for success—as benchmarking enables fast-track evaluation, which drives the school improvement process that occurs in a broader—systems—environment.

Everaert, in an article written for the Drucker Foundation book *The Organization of the Future* entitled "Emotions, Tempo, and Timing in Managing People,"[51] defines appropriate benchmarking processes for the new millennium. The steps outlined are as follows:

1. Know your current position. Before defining any new direction and planning or replanning the future, you need an honest assessment of where you are today. Without that, filling pages on where you are going tomorrow is like jumping in the water from a ten-foot diving board without knowing which way it is pointing, how high it is, or even how much water is in the pool.
2. Benchmark your achievements against those of the industry. Benchmarking must be realistic. Too many organizations still compare themselves to themselves . . .
3. Benchmark your long-term plan (LTP). Compare your goals for your organization to where you believe others in your industry will be three or four years down the road. Ask these questions:
    3a. If we are successful and achieve all of our LTP goals, where will we stand compared to our competitors?
    3b. Will they have taken a still bigger leap forward?
    3c. Will they have raised the standards of the industry to higher levels?
4. Will your industry or trade survive in the future?

In setting school and district achievement goals, these are useful steps to follow. First, we need to know how well our students are doing on reasonably valid and reliable measures of achievement. As for the future of the "testing" movement, there is little question where this is going. The political movement that has so gripped this country shows no sign of loosing its grip on state and national educational policy.[52-55] Consequently, we will no doubt see states continue to mandate tougher and tougher mastery tests. And there is now a possibility of having a national test of student achievement. As the standards for those measures rise, those schools that do not keep pace will fall further and further behind. (An excellent resource for information on goals and standards is the National Science Foundation Web site at www.nsf.gov and *Raising the Standard*.[56])

Second, schools need to determine how well they are doing against so-called industry standards. These take the form of content standards for each subject matter developed by various governmental agencies and or professional organizations and by states that mandate tough mastery tests. (For example, approaches and standards that are being developed to systematically evaluate various instructional areas beyond the basic three Rs: see "National Study of School Evaluation," http://ozzy.interaccess.com/nsse/ioq.html.) Determining the difference between local performance levels and appropriate standards establishes performance targets for improvement.

Next, schools should project three to four years by asking themselves if their performance targets will keep pace with state goals and the progress made in other districts. This is not an issue of competition, but one of providing the best possible education for their students. Putting plans in place today that will result in learning levels that are deficient four years from now is just not sound practice and is not in the best interest of students. Consequently, it is imperative that these performance targets be as far-reaching as possible. To make this point, Tom Peters[57] warns of the possible limitations of benchmarking:

> What is genuine excellence? It's Michael Jordan. No one has . . . EVER . . . played the game the way he does. He's taken it to a new level. More than that: He has reinvented basketball.
>
> It's my problem with benchmarking. Benchmark against "the best." But that evades the biggest issue: Those who really make a difference create a . . . whole new way . . . of doing business (basketball!) in their part of the market. Invent whole new markets. Best of the best? That wasn't Netscape's approach to the Internet. They wanted to "be the only ones who do what we do." Jerry Garcia would have been proud! This, of course, is the "analytic point of the book and my chief economic argument: Innovation/Just Say No to Commodity? Just Say Yes to Wow!"

If we take Peters's advice, we will work to establish improvement targets that are far-reaching and exciting, yet doable. Why doable? Because people need to know that there is a reasonable chance of achieving those goals or they will give up and not even try—losing confidence in their leadership. Overzealous goals and initiatives that extend beyond the ability of the organization to realistically achieve them will not be embraced, and leaders who persist do so at personal risk of failure. That's because it is just not possible to *truly* lead a democratic organization without cultivating followers for any length of time. For example, an inner city school performing at the 5th percentile on the state mastery test *will not* be at the 80th percentile in three years. That's unrealistic, and everyone knows it. But setting a short-term, three-year goal of being within the third quartile (50th to the 75th percentile) should be doable. So, in this case, the long-term goal becomes "high achievement for all students" or "all students can learn at high levels." However, the operational, short-term goal is more incremental. (This may seem contradictory to my statement earlier about setting targets that are meaningful three to four years down the road so as to not render students deficient. It is not as the issue here is: what is appropriate and challenging, given current levels of performance? School leaders have to balance what is desired in the long run versus what is doable in the short term. That process necessitates knowing baseline performance levels, comparing that to the end-goal, and setting doable and meaningful incremental targets to get there. In cases where baseline performance is very low, it will take time to reach high standards. In cases where students are underperforming, as discussed in previous chapters, maintaining mediocre performance by virtue of inappropriate and low targets is wrong. Thus, there is a need for decision-making here that is based on informed intuition. The process of setting these targets is as much an art as it is a science. I argue in this book that it should be neither just art nor science, but that decision-makers need both to reach the best possible conclusion.)

Finally, Everaert asks a fourth question: "Will your industry or trade survive in the future?" This may seem a curious question for educators to ponder since schools seem so entrenched in American society. Nonetheless, we should remember that the single greatest growth market in education today is home schooling. In addition, the charter movement is making great strides in many states and cities. So this question may not be so far-fetched after all.

Systems Thinking Methodology and a "Helicopter View"

Systems thinking does have a methodology, but it is complex and broad-based—there are no quick answers here for those who prefer how-to lists. Senge et al.[58] reference a wide array or tools and methods to help one make sense of and draw order from the organizational complexity:

> At its broadest level, systems thinking encompasses a large and fairly amorphous body of methods, tools, and principles, all looking at the inter-relatedness of forces, and seeing them as part of a common process.

Senge and colleagues[59] further explain:

> The discipline of systems thinking is the study of system structure and behaviour; it is enriched by a set of tools and techniques that have developed over the past thirty-five years, particularly since the advent of powerful computers. People who have experience with systems thinking can act with more effective leverage than a "short-attention-span culture" generally permits.

To explain what one does when practicing systems thinking, O'Connor and McDermott[60] refer to using feedback loops and thinking in circles. The importance of feedback loops is emphasized throughout the TQM and leadership literature.[61–73] For our purposes in helping us understand, for example, how staff development affects curriculum development, O'Connor and McDermott[74] explain it best:

> Systems thinking is thinking in loops rather than in straight lines. The parts of a system are all connected directly or indirectly, therefore a change in one part ripples out to affect all the other parts. So, these other parts will change, and the effect of this will ripple out in turn to affect the original part. The original then responds to that new influence. Therefore the influence comes back to the original part in a modified way, making a loop, not a one-way street. This is called a *feedback loop*. When two parts are connected, influences can go both ways, like a telephone line—if you can dial a friend, they can equally well dial you. Feedback is the output of a system re-entering as its input, or the return of information to influence the next step.

Schools and the people in them need regular feedback to help them do their jobs and meet the goals of the organization. Feedback changes that "ripple" through the organization can come back to affect the original goal in unexpected ways. It is for this very reason that data-driven decision-making should be used within a systems environment. Data-driven decision-making is just a set of tools—it is not an end in and of itself, and it must not be conducted in a vacuum. It should be practiced within the context and purpose of providing feedback for continual improvement. As staff are provided that feedback, their perceptions and understandings about "what is" can change from their original understandings and intents, hence the need for a systems thinking approach and a helicopter view.

No doubt our efforts will be improved if feedback systems can be strengthened. As Figure 6.8 shows, as we measure outcomes and make instructional changes, feedback systems should constantly provide staff with information about what effects the changes are having and help them consider what additional changes might be needed along the way.

Thus, the first goal of improvement should focus on building an organizational infrastructure that enables fast-tack evaluation for feedback purposes and then to use that information to better understand what is occurring throughout the organization—using systems thinking.

A systems thinking methodology useful for school improvement is best summed up by Gharajedaghi.[75] To help "see" what is happening among all the interrelated parts of the organization, Gharajedaghi suggests we use holistic inquiry focusing on structure, function, and process.

> Structure defines component parts and their relationships, which in this context is synonymous with input, means, and cause. Function defines the outcome, or results produced, which is also synonymous with outputs, ends, and effect. Process explicitly defines the sequence of activities and the know-how required to produce the outcomes. Structure, function, and process, along with their containing environment, form the *interdependent* set of variables that define the whole. (110)

Taking these operational definitions and applying them to our work, *structure* refers to the people who carry out various processes within the school. Teachers deliver instruction, curriculum planners and developers design the curriculum and select materials, and professional development trainers help bridge

Feeback Loops for "An Integrated Systems Approach to School Improvement"

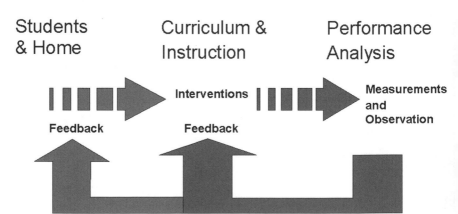

Figure 6.8   Importance of Feedback for Systems Thinking

the gap between those who plan curriculum and those who carry it out. Principals manage and lead all that goes on in their buildings. Parents can help bridge the learning gaps between home and school, coordinating their children's education and providing critical motivation and support for learning. Superintendents help design the strategic direction of the organization with their boards and coordinate activities and resources. They manage the politics of the organization and secure budgets to carry out the district's mission with the assistance of their budget administrators. *Process*, on the other hand, refers to "how we do what we do" and, for the purposes of this book, the "how" relates to the data-driven decision-making process within a framework of fast-track evaluation. *Function* refers to "what is being produced" and, for education, that is learning. The application of these concepts to education can be summed up with the two charts shown in Figures 6.4 and 6.6.

To manage and make sense of all this complexity (sometimes seen as chaos), enhanced leadership skills will be needed. Not only must school leaders be proficient in the processes of education, they must also be able to navigate the various structures at work and be able to understand the implications of various output measures as function is considered against the original goals. These are not linear issues; they are multidimensional and complex and require effective feedback loops for success. All of this must be led by people who Mojkowski, my colleague, and I refer to as having a helicopter view of their organization, thus knowing what it needs for meaningful change.

Planning

No one would argue with the need for systematic and thoughtful planning for organizational success, but the key is in the effectiveness of that planning process. In the systems model proposed here, planning to be most effective should be conducted *after* information on program evaluation is reported. In this regard, systems' processes are linear because it makes little sense for planning to proceed without knowing "where we are today," which is an evaluation function. We have discussed examples earlier where project implementation has led to changes both in the need for further analysis and the modification of plans, but at the outset, this relationship between evaluation and planning should be thought of as linear.

For example, we would want to have conducted an evaluation of several programs before establishing long-term district or school goals to improve achievement, as doing so helps establish priorities. To accomplish this, analyses of program performance would be necessary to identify the areas most in need of improvement measured against standards we feel are appropriate to measure success. Thus, if these analyses were to point to the need for improving science achievement at the high school level, for example, appropriate steps would then be planned and implemented that could include both curricular and instructional changes. In arriving at this conclusion to focus on science, we might conduct a review of course-taking trends and standardized test results along with the careers of graduates. Once a decision is made to focus on science, financial and human resources would be allocated through the planning process.

But what would happen if, through the course of these program evaluation analyses, we found that the root problem was not with the existing science curriculum, but rather with the prerequisite math course taking policy. Sometimes a policy such as this forces all but the most advanced students to be eliminated from algebra in eighth grade, leaving them to take algebra in ninth grade and subsequently causing them to miss out on the advanced science course sequence in tenth, eleventh, and twelfth grades. This finding would then be fed back to both the math and science departments to discuss options and solutions.

In summary, then, at the outset, there is a linear relationship between evaluation and planning, and it is important to conduct as much research as is reasonable and practical before conducting the planning process. Then, as the entire systems process unfolds, there will be times when feedback from implementation reveals unforeseen problems needing attention.

Reactive, Proactive, and Interactive Planning

As we have seen, the planning process should be dynamic and flexible. Gharajedaghi[76] refers to three types of planning: reactive, proactive, and interactive. While reactive planning "is concerned with identifying deficiencies and designing projects and strategies to remove or suppress them," proactive planning focuses on "prediction and preparation." In their important book on the superintendency, Cunningham and Carter[77] make numerous references to how superintendents deal with issues and pressures that affect organizational health and performance. Most of the activities that they describe can be categorized as either reactive or proactive planning, while others reflect what Gharajedaghi refers to as interactive planning, "which assumes that the future is created by what we and others do between now and then." Senge et al.[78] make reference to this same notion—the idealization of the future—as one of the five learning disciplines—"shared vision" where "people with common purpose (e.g., the teachers, administrators, and staff in a school) can learn to nourish a sense of commitment in a group or organization by developing shared images of the future they seek to create and the principles and guiding practices by which they hope to get there." To become most effective, these images need to be turned into plans for implementation. Therefore, in one sense, the objective here is to design a desirable future (idealization) and to invent or select ways of bringing it about (realization). Gharajedaghi[79] goes on to say that "systems methodology rests on the interactive type of planning." In this sense, planning is ongoing, a part of the integration of the various parts or subsystems of the larger system we call a school system.

Earlier, Senge et al.[80] made a distinction between traditional planning, often conducted within each of the subsystems of the organization, and a broader view that incorporates systems thinking. In referring to the budget process, which is so critical to the success of any organization, he noted that these processes conducted independently of one another (budget separate from other processes) provide little or "no opportunity to talk about creative ideas, corporate purpose, vision, or commitment" (81). Instead, he used the phrase "developing a learning organization" to better describe the interplay among the various structures and processes of the organization of which planning is critical. This is why Franzi (see chapter 5) argues that budgets must first and foremost help achieve district goals. Planning of the type that enables a learning organization must be "joint-planning," or what Gharajedaghi describes as interactive planning.

Steven Covey, the noted leadership and organizational expert, addresses this issue as well. Covey, Merrill, and Merrill,[81] like Gardner[82] before them, are concerned about the alignment of structures and systems for organizational success, arguing that without this alignment organizational purposes will not be attained. They are also interested in "strategic orientation" as they recall this exchange with Masaharu Matsushita, president of Japan's giant consumer electronic company, when Matsushita claimed, "We are going to win, and the industrial West is going to lose because the reasons for your failure are within yourselves: for you, the essence of management is to get the ideas out of the heads of the bosses into the hands of labor." Covey and colleagues reflect:

> The important thing here is the stated reason for our "failure." We are locked in to certain mind-sets or paradigms, locked in to management by maps, locked in to an old model of leadership where the experts at the top decide the objectives, methods, and means.
>
> This old strategic planning model is obsolete. It's a road map. It calls for people at the top to exercise their experience, expertise, wisdom, and judgment and set

ten-year strategic plans—only to find that the plans are worthless within eighteen months. In the new environment . . . plans become obsolete fast. (98)

Bill Creech, author of *The Five Pillars of Total Quality Management*, quality guru and past commander of the Tactical Air Command of the U.S. Air Force, reflects on what it took to reshape the strategic air command that inevitably played such as important role in the Gulf War.

> It was not obvious to Americans in those dramatic opening hours, but the overall tone of the air campaign had been set. Purposeful professionalism, operating in the framework—all with the accumulated benefits—of a *quality* approach to all aspects of the demanding business of air combat was to prove its worth again and again in the stressful days that followed. That quality approach encompassed all the elements required for success; there were no weak links. It embraced the *people*, the *equipment*, the *training*, the *planning*, the *strategy*, the *tactics*—and especially the approach to *organization* and *leadership* that had to pull all of those elements together into a collective and focused team effort. Those multiple factors, operating interactively, were not fully appreciated by most outside observers. (119)

The main point here is that planning should not be considered something done every two or three years, or every summer in an administrative retreat. While that sounds so much like a cliché, the fact is that this is what many of us still practice. Planning needs to be ongoing—it is integral to every other process in the organization. As the organization changes, so too must its plans, literally by virtue of the fact that the organization has changed. This seems so obvious, but it's hard to implement because often the changes are subtle and, as we are so busy once plans are set with our boards, we tend to ignore them for a period of time. But these plans do need updating and changing, which is why plans at the administrative level should be flexible. Formal strategic planning had a noble goal—to engage many constituents in the development of the plan. And formally, these plans were intended to be reviewed yearly. But that was often not the practice. This is why Tom Peters has said that: "Plans are worthless, but planning is invaluable." In the integrated systems approach model for school improvement, organizational goals and objectives are developed as give and take between program evaluation (fast-track evaluation) and the planning processes. Moreover, we know that what we learn through implementation can often cause a need to change the plans. Thus, plans can become outdated almost the minute they are written—as staff within the organization (structure) react to ongoing organizational change. This all points to the need for interactive planning.

Leadership for an Effective Organization

We now come to the crux of the issue: What are the leadership characteristics and skills that will enable this new way of systems thinking to take hold and positively affect school environments?

If effective organizations are characterized by strong relationships among people and systems of people, then forging and nurturing those relationships becomes the artistry and prowess of expert leadership. When I think about the leadership experience of my most capable colleagues, words I use to describe them are "visionary, relationship builders, trusting, instilling confidence, enabling the talents of others, demanding but fair, friendly and likeable." Effective leaders are, at the same time, passionate about people and student learning. They lead by building trust and engendering respect and a desire on the part of the people in their organization to do the right thing. Their leadership is focused on student learning and the success of kids. They know the difference between delegating and leading, and they surround themselves with the best and the brightest and provide them the latitude and freedom to act tactically. However, for the strategic decisions (those overarching issues that deal with setting direction for the school system), effective leaders rightfully retain final decision-making for themselves and their boards. By virtue of the position they hold, only they can see the "big picture" because they have the knowledge and the helicopter view to know what is right and what needs to be done for overall improvement. Effective leaders also possess a sense of humor and often laugh at themselves publicly. This demonstrates that they are real people and that they have the self-confidence to put their flaws out in the open for everyone to see.

A recruiter I recently spoke with used the phrase "good people" to sum up a certain individual. I don't use management skills such as organizational ability, fiscal strength, or planner to describe what these "experts" do. These managerial skills are assumed; they are the foundations of expert leadership. On the other hand, someone who is a fiscal expert, planner, or who is highly organized may not be a good leader. Bill Spady[83] reflects on his early thinking about leadership, noting that "leaders initiate improvements and get results—all the rest . . . we asserted, was details." Thirty years of practice, research, trial, and error have, I believe, proved him right. Finally, when the attributes of relationship building are added to the requisite managerial skills, we rise to a different level of understanding and practice of leadership. Peters[84] stresses this point:

> What does it take to lead an organization of businesspersons? "In essence, the leadership challenge is to provide the 'glue' to cohere independent units in a world

characterized by forces of entropy and fragmentation. Only one element has been identified as powerful enough to overcome the centrifugal forces, and that is trust."—Jim O'Toole, author of *Leading Change*

In my seminars, I pause when I get to this quote. I spend a few minutes on it, then I announce, "Everything I have said before, everything I will subsequently say, hinges on this one, single remark."

Why? I think O'Toole gets it exactly right. He's addressing *the* paradox of our age. It's a paradox futurist John Naisbitt addressed, too, in his seminal book *Megatrends*. Naisbit talked about "high tech, high touch." Meaning . . . paradoxically . . . the higher the tech and the more dispersed the networks, the more important the touch or . . . per O'Toole . . . trust. How about this: *high tech, high trust.*

Specifically, what is it that school leaders do, and how do they do it? Are there *any* models we can look to for guidance? Mojkowski and I use the term *helicopter view* to describe the leader's ability to navigate in and among the complexity and chaos that often characterize our organizations. My early training was in music, and I had the great fortune to play in an orchestra for a time and to do some conducting as a school and community band director. The following example[85] works better than any other for me in helping to describe what great (school) leaders do:

What can we learn about business (leadership) from a coach or conductor? The wonderful news for the football coach: He can't throw the ball as well as his quarterback. Can't block as well as his left tackle. And the conductor? Can't play the violin nearly as well as his first violinist. Thus, the coach/conductor has a-b-s-o-l-u-t-e-l-y no alternative but to develop others. It's develop others . . . or else.

. . . That is, the essence of great coaching/playing and directing/acting (Martin Scorsese and Robert De Niro in *Raging Bull)* is . . . ALWAYS . . . stretching beyond what is imaginable. That is . . . it's all about innovation.

Or put another way, the next performance . . . somewhere on earth . . . of Mozart's fabulous 41st ("Jupiter") is probably the 202,423rd performance of that symphony. But what will make it special, in the hands of a modern-day Leonard Bernstein, is that the 202,423rd interpretation is new/original/fresh . . . even though, in one (very) limited sense, it's true to the original score.

Coaching and conducting and direction are about . . . innovating . . . about originality . . . about freshness . . . or, as I like to say, about loose and tight.

Excellence . . . and I'll be the first to acknowledge it . . . really is about loose and tight: the most creative activities (symphony, theater, sports, surgery) demand loose and tight.

Visa founder, Dee Hock, talks about systems that combine chaos and order. Within the Visa family, for example, a few basics must be executed with absolute precision. On the other hand, members are free/encouraged to improvise on many marketing dimensions.

Loose. Tight. Combine the two. Chaos and order. "Chaordic," per Dee Hock. Life. Tight is good! (Great.) Loose is good! (Great.) The two are complements, not either/or, not enemies." (Peters 1977, 150–151)

Sergiovanni[86] speaks to achieving a balance between the "lifeworld" of leadership, focusing on "culture, meaning and significance" and the "systemsworld" that describes the organizational structures or "instrumentalities," as he puts it. He argues persuasively that there must be a balance between these two, that "when things are working the way they should in a school, the lifeworld and systemsworld engage each other in a symbiotic relationship" but that the systemsworld must be driven by the goals of the lifeworld.

Two works focusing on leadership and the superintendency have influenced many aspiring and practicing superintendents, but the principles they discuss apply to all school leaders, regardless of level. Cunningham and Carter's[87] *The American School Superintendent: Leading in an Age of Pressure* looks at the pressures of modern day school district leaders, noting example after example of effective practice. It is clear that what it takes to be successful today is different from what it took only ten years ago. Not better—different. This idea is key because it affects the preparation and skill set required for effective school district leadership in the new millennium. Johnson's[88] *Leading to Change: The Challenge of the New Superintendency* follows the growth and development of new superintendents exploring the nature of leadership and its development. Both books explore practices of successful superintendents. Johnson explores those new to the field, while Cunningham and Carter examine the best in practice today across America. In taking this journey of best practice, they must also explore what does not work as well. As I said earlier, the planning models used throughout school districts today often do not fulfill their promises, for reasons already discussed. That is a systems issue. Effective school leaders get beyond this limitation just as a good symphony conductor gets beyond a weak musician (somehow the Hartford Symphony and its conductor made great music despite this rather average bassoonist!). The best practices that Cunningham and Carter and Johnson describe mirror what Peters and others espouse about effective leadership.

While the skills of leadership can be taught, leadership is also developed over time as a function of experience within organizational relationships. For example, it is impossible in my opinion to "teach" someone how to lead a school district as a superintendent if he or she has not already led an organization—a school for example—as a principal. We can teach *about* it, but one can't add deep meaning to that experience because the relationships they have had with others throughout their organizational work history have not been sufficiently broad. Maxwell[89] notes this truism as his "Third Irrefutable Law of Leadership—The Law of Process: Leadership Develops Daily, Not in a Day." This is why I refer to relationship and capacity building as the artistry and prowess of expert leadership. We can teach the content of leadership, but artistry and prowess are gained over time and with experience.

There are many models of leadership that should not be left out of this discussion—too many to review extensively, as this is not the purpose of this book. However, in reviewing the literature, especially that of the closing decade during which organizations so dramatically changed, requiring a "new leadership," there has emerged a clear difference between what leaders and managers "do," as well as what characterizes successful leaders "as people" from those who are less successful.[90–106]

Leadership characteristics, that is, the characteristics successful leaders possess that can be gleaned from the thousands of case studies explored through the volumes noted above, can be summed up as:

1. Trustworthiness
2. Honorability, morality, high integrity
3. Resilience
4. Willingness to empower and distribute authority
5. Expectation for self and others
6. Intuition
7. Flexibility

In fact, the single most noted characteristic for effective leadership is trust—bar none. Gardner,[107] the father of modern day leadership, explains this point when he notes that:

> In a sense, leadership is confirmed by followers. To say that followers have substantial influence on leaders sounds like the view of someone steeped in the democratic tradition. . . .
>
> Contemporary research confirms the two-way character of the relationship. It is this reciprocal aspect that underlies one of the soundest political maxims: *good constituents tend to produce good leaders*.

If successful leadership rests on the relationship between leader and follower, then trust is at the heart of that relationship. Trust in any relationship comes first. Perhaps this is why "change agent" and "clean house" type school/district leaders may solve short-term problems, but their long-term effect on the organization is often more damaging as a whole. Finally, trust must be based on something deeper—a true belief that the people in your organization will do what is right. Gardner states:

> If one is leading, teaching, dealing with young people or engaged in any other activity that involves influencing, directing, guiding, helping, or nurturing, the whole tone of the relationship is conditioned by one's faith in human possibilities.
>
> When the faith is present in the leader, it communicates itself to followers with powerful effect. *In the conventional mode people want to know whether the followers believe in the leader; a more searching question is whether the leader believes in the followers.* (199)

We have found that this basic characteristic of leadership—developing a trusting culture—is also critical at the school level for success. Sebring and Bryk's[108] research in Chicago on the role of the principal in guiding change focuses on this trust as the foundation upon which all else is built:

> SOCIAL TRUST: THE FOUNDATION FOR SCHOOL DEVELOPMENT. Formal structures provide only the skeleton of a productive school. How people behave, interact, learn, and work together is what breathes life into a school. Schools that are improving are characterized by co-operative work relations among all adults. To achieve this state requires a strong base of social trust among teachers, between teachers and parents, between teachers and the principal, and between teachers and students. In schools that are improving, where trust and cooperative adult efforts are strong, students also report that they feel safe, sense that teachers care about them, and experience greater academic challenge. In contrast, in schools with flat or declining test scores, teachers are more likely to state they do not trust one another, and both teachers and students report less satisfaction with their experiences.

These fundamental concepts of trust, morality, relationship, belief in the human spirit, resilience, sharing of power and authority, and building organizational capacity for change are the foundation—the building blocks—on which sound leadership practice is built.

The skills of leadership, on the other hand, are different. These skills describe what effective leaders do and not what characterizes their personalities. In my view, these skills are necessary but insufficient conditions for success in today's complex organizations. While it may be possible to practice these skills without the character set noted above, it is unlikely that long-term success will be achieved. The skills of leadership emerging over and over again in the literature are:

1. Focusing on mission
2. Building agreement among staff

3. Institution building; paying attention to interdependence (systems interdependence)
4. Exercise of nonjurisdictional power
5. Knowledge and use of effective motivation techniques
6. Ability to clearly explain issues
7. Knowledge and expertise

Two works in particular summarize these leadership issues well (characteristics and skills): one in the private sector and the other in education. *The Leader of the Future*[109] is an anthology of best thinking on leadership practice. *Total Leaders: Applying the Best Future-Focused Change Strategies to Education*[110] takes what we have learned in leadership over the past twenty years or so and applies it to best practices for education.

Yet the model that comes closest to pulling *all* of this together for me is Margaret Wheatley's[111] *Leadership and the New Science: Learning about Organization from an Orderly Universe*. Wheatley writes:

> Leadership, an amorphous phenomenon that has intrigued us since people began studying organizations, is being examined now for its relational aspects. More and more studies focus on followership, empowerment, and leader accessibility. And ethical and moral questions are no longer fuzzy religious concepts but key elements in our relationships with staff, suppliers, and stakeholders. If the physics of our universe is revealing the primacy of relationships (reference to quantum physics), is it any wonder that we are beginning to reconfigure our ideas about management in relational terms?
>
> . . . The impact of vision, values, and culture occupies a great deal of organizational attention. . . . Many scientists now work with the concept of fields—invisible forces that structure space or behavior. I have come to understand organizational vision as a field—a force of unseen connections that influence employees' behavior—rather than as an evocative message about some desired future state.
>
> . . . We have begun to speak in earnest of more fluid, organic structures, even of boundaryless organizations. We are beginning to recognize organizations as systems, construing them as "learning organizations" and crediting them with some type of self-renewing capacity. (12–13)

For those school leaders who see only chaos and have difficulty creating a vision from the "fields" that make up their organizations, change and improvement will be slow. Changes that do occur in these settings will likely be driven by outside influences. The effective school leaders that Cunningham and Carter[112] and Johnson[113] write about not only perceive these fields, but also can derive sense from the chaos and lead their organizations toward commonly defined goals. These leaders possess an ability to see the whole and to make sense and order of the stream of data and problems coming at them from every quarter, every minute of the day. They possess and expertly use the skills of leadership, but they also see a broader view of the multitude of interrelated systems, people, and needs and can focus and work within all of this complexity to serve the interests of their students.

Finally, a word on what all this has to do with data-driven decision-making. A consistent theme of this book is that data-driven decision-making is not something that is performed in a vacuum—it is a tool set for use in improving decision-making within a larger set of organizational subsystems and their component structures, functions, and processes. Wheatley[114] captures this theme nicely:

> Participation and relationships are only part of our present dilemmas. Here we sit in the Information Age, besieged by more information than any mind can handle, trying to make sense of the complexity that continues to grow around us. Is information anything more than a new and perplexing management tool?
>
> In organizations, we aren't suffering from information overload just because of technology, and we won't get out from under our information dilemmas just by using more sophisticated information-sorting technologies. Something much bigger is being asked of us. We are moving irrevocably into a new relationship with the creative force of nature. However long we may drag our feet, we will be forced to accept that information—freely generated and freely exchanged—is our only hope for organization. If we fail to recognize its generative properties, we will be unable to manage in this new world.

Peters[115] says:

> The information technology—no matter how powerful—is "merely" an ENABLER. You can wire yourself up until you are blue in the face (and broke) . . . but in the end it's a people game.

No doubt data-driven decision-making is an important skill for helping drive improvement. But we must be careful not to become so enamored with the technology so as to lose sight of the bigger, more important reality that the interrelationships among the various systems that make up our organizations and with those who work in them are what improvement will be built upon.

Professional Development and Evaluation

Just as composer, musician, and conductor come together to put on a great performance, school improvement occurs with implementation. And we must never lose site of the fact that it is our teachers and administrators who carry out and implement improvement plans. Without them, all we have is a set of goals and plans, so it behooves schools to provide the best training to assist teachers and administrators in their roles. Then, over time, we need to hold staff professionally accountable for their work in the most positive sense of the word. Since the topics of systems implementation, other than data-driven decision-making, are beyond the scope of this book, I will provide just a brief overview of the main issues of concern in implementing professional development activities within an integrated systems approach to school improvement.

The main purpose of conducting professional development activities should be to assist teachers in gaining new knowledge about innovative and effective instructional materials and techniques and helping to apply them in their classrooms. It is almost universally agreed that, to be effective, staff development activities need to be contextual (i.e., tied directly to experiences that teachers have and need).[116, 117] However, in practice, we continue to deliver the lion's share of staff development in large, lecture formats that are far less than productive. The delivery of staff development in ways that take most advantage of contextual meaning requires new models and different approaches. The following example will help bring these issues into focus.

A few years ago, a school district wanted to change from its old language arts materials to the more effective "integrated" language arts approach in grades K–6. Their first implementation step was to buy the new materials and provide typical training in large, school/grade-based groups. That is, after large group introductions of the materials (this approach is fine for basic introductions and overviews), teachers from grade one met monthly with a "trainer," as did teachers from each grade, and this process was duplicated across the district's elementary schools. At first glance, this approach seems to be contextual, as teachers were meeting by grade and school level to deal with their small group issues. However, the main problem they encountered was that the effective delivery of an integrated language arts program requires faculty who possess a breadth of experience and knowledge in reading, language arts, and children's literature. This is not a problem that breaks down nicely into cohorts of grade levels. It is more specifically a teacher knowledge and experience issue. This district showed no appreciable improvement in holistic writing scores or reading levels after two years of professional development work. Concerned, the superintendent brought teachers together to ask what might be wrong, and the answer was immediately forthcoming. Teachers knew what the problem was—teaching integrated language arts effectively is hard to accomplish because one must not only possess a great repertoire of knowledge, but also must be able to diagnose reading problems "on the fly." After some discussion, a whole new approach to professional development was taken, but one that also required *organizational* change. It was decided that a handful of local teacher experts (agreed to by faculty consent) would (1) design instructional lessons appropriate to this district, (2) be freed from all duties and extra assignments, and (3) be provided a teacher aide to help them work with the other teachers in their school dealing with specific, contextual teaching problems. After two years of these combined efforts, student achievement rose in both writing and reading.

This superintendent made a critical leadership decision as this new approach to implementation was being developed. She stated that moving forward with the implementation of an integrated language arts program was not negotiable, citing research and best practice indicating that this was the preferred method of instruction. But she also recognized that it took new skill sets to succeed. Therefore, she offered to remove "time" from the accountability agenda. She stated that, while district and individual progress was nonnegotiable, the district would stay with it for as long as it took to get results. In the end, it did not take long at all, but the offer to extend the time factor turned out to be critical. Thus, she changed the ground rules for accountability through this growth and development phase. Negative evaluations would only result now if a teacher decided not to participate—errors of commission. Stressing research and best practice, recognizing that this approach would be difficult for many teachers to implement, as they had taught using traditional methods for so many years, she backed up this commitment with action by making needed systems changes, thereby all but assuring buy-in and success.

Obviously, there was a good deal of give and take in this example between and among all the components/systems of an integrated systems approach to school improvement. Through ongoing program evaluation, it was determined that the new approaches and materials were not having the intended effect. Discussions with principals and teachers confirmed the reasons. New plans had to be developed, and organizational structures changed that affected staffing, budgets, and school assignments in order to implement the revised professional development plans. Also, it was critical that the superintendent take the position that her people wanted to do their best, to do what was right, but that the current system was not helping them.

All of this activity requires resources. A recent study by Killeen and Monk[118] indicates that school districts allocate somewhere between 1 and 3 percent of their budgets to professional development. This study also shows that a large percent of these funds go for materials and activities that we would not normally consider as staff development, such as library/media re-sources. This figure of between 1 and 3 percent falls far short of what the private sector spends on training, but to lament this fact will not change it significantly. What we need are creative, innovative approaches to how these resources are allocated. We have learned that staff development activities should be contextual, based on real problems for participants and not contrived examples, and that these activities need to be ongoing and systematic (i.e., that they should be planned through feedback from the other critical school systems). And, when necessary, organizational changes need to be made to facilitate change led by thoughtful and sensitive school leaders.

Personnel Evaluation Systems

A colleague recently lamented that, after years of practice and research, we have no hard evidence that our personnel evaluation systems make any real or meaningful difference in the lives of staff or the effectiveness of school organizations. Having spent a good deal of time in this field myself, I tend to agree, but there are examples where evaluation matters. Thus we must develop the most effective accountability system possible. The old discussions of the role and importance of evaluation versus supervision and what we do as a result are not the subject of this discussion. I will leave it to the reader to determine where that line between helping and evaluating "for the record" lies. Instead, my purpose is to discuss the importance of accountability systems and to promote what we have come to recognize as "best practice," even if those best practices are yet to be clearly defined through research.

The challenge in developing an effective evaluation system is in explicating what outstanding teachers and administrators do. Take, for example, the list of leader characteristics and skills discussed earlier in this chapter. While we may be able to assess whether our principals are focusing on mission, building agreement among staff, building capacity within the institution by virtue of paying attention to system interdependence, and so on, it is much more difficult to measure the application of these skills through the characteristics of trust, honor, morality, resiliency, empowerment, expectations, intuition, and flexibility. We know it when we see it, but trying to explicate it in sufficient detail for a personnel evaluation system is extremely difficult.

Recently, I was discussing superintendent leadership issues with a doctoral student, trying to nail down his dissertation purpose and problem. We were discussing the value of using lists of leadership competencies, such as the joint draft by AASA and the National School Boards Association or the Interstate School Leaders Licensure Consortium,[119] as a template for the skill sets needed for success and contract renewal. As we were talking, I began to think about the superintendents I know and reminded myself that what they do exemplifies something more than what is on those lists—as the "sum" of what they do is greater than the simple collection of skills and characteristics listed. They possess and use a helicopter view, and they know when and how to get out of the helicopter— knowing when to get involved with detail, when to get above it. This has everything to do with Wheatley's "fields" and knowing what to do based on the ability to perceive almost imperceptible shifts in systems dynamics. Teaching and leading are more than lists of competencies, which is why my colleague argues that we have little hard research to prove that all of this activity with personnel evaluation has had any effect on our institutional success. Thus, my graduate student moved from using the lists on a survey to doing in-depth interviews to get at the richness and complexity of school district leadership.

Unfortunately, the technical systems for making these assessments more valid and reliable have just not developed to the point where our knowledge and beliefs lie—beliefs based on what research does exist and our observations about what constitutes effective leadership practice. By the same token, we will not find anyone who would argue that assessment and accountability are unimportant parts of a larger system.

The same problems exist in teacher evaluation. Two outstanding models for what to look for exist in David Berliner's conception of "pedagogical-content knowledge"[120] and Saphier and Gower's *The Skillful Teacher*.[121] There are others, but Berliner[122] and Saphier and Gower clearly hit the mark best. The instructional problem discussed earlier of the school district that was trying to implement an integrated language arts program was that most of their teachers were not "pedagogical-content" experts in this area. And, as Berliner has taught us, you do not make a pedagogical-content expert overnight—it takes time and extensive experience. Although not purposefully, Saphier and Gower come closest to explicating what it is that pedagogical-content experts do, but even here they do not capture the essence or gestalt of teaching. Banner and Cannon[123] do so in their book on the elements of teaching. Their list of teacher competencies looks very different than previous lists, as they include the desire for learning, authority gained by knowledge and presence, ethics, order, imagination, compassion, patience, character, taking and demonstrating pleasure from the act of teaching. Although it is easy to agree with this list, it is hard to systematically and accurately evaluate many of these qualities such as authority, ethics, imagination, compassion, and pleasure. So while we may be able to describe the essence of teaching, our system of teacher evaluation most often falls far short of being able to provide adequate analysis and feedback to teachers about their performance and skills. This is why teacher evaluation is now moving to the practice of using portfolios to gain a richer, fuller picture of what the teacher is doing in the classroom.

If function matters in systems thinking and organizational effectiveness, then assessing and holding accountable those who work within the system (to be sure that the process gets implemented) is critical. From a helping perspective and then from an accountability perspective, evaluation is important for those fundamentally unwilling or unable to perform. It is also important to acknowledge good work, as everyone needs and wants feedback on their performance, measured against organizational expectations. In sum, this is why I include personnel evaluation as part of the larger system needed for school improvement, even though the technical problems in conducting effective evaluation are challenging. Of all the systems I have discussed, personnel evaluation is the one we know how to do least well. Perhaps it's best that we acknowledge the limitations of current best practice and move forward from there. Even portfolio evaluation, while better than using lists, is still problematic, as it takes an inordinate amount of time to conduct, thereby affecting other systems. Regardless—personnel evaluation does need to be conducted.

To date, most of our teacher and administrator evaluation activities are driven by state-mandated approaches, which, of necessity, focus on lists of competencies validated as important for success and supported by the research literature. There are even nationally developed lists, especially for administration/leadership, published by Council of Chief State School Officers (1996) and AASA (1994). As discussed earlier, many of these competency lists are implemented as lists are so often—disjointed, the parts without the whole. It is unfair and really not possible to effectively assess teachers' (and administrators') performance without holistically addressing factors such as motivation in concert with selection of teaching materials and development of lesson plans. Great teaching, like great leadership, cannot be dissected and analyzed in pieces—for the whole is greater than the sum of the parts. For now, at least, we are left with the state of the art as it exists, and we need to use what we have until new approaches to teacher evaluation are more fully developed. Specifically, portfolio approaches have the potential to capture both the gestalt and the detail needed for improvement and formal evaluation. Perhaps the overall best resource in addressing all of these critical issues in teacher evaluation is *Evaluating Teaching: A Guide to Current Thinking and Best Practice*, edited by James Stronge.[124] Here we can learn the state of the art in teacher evaluation systems (with the previously discussed limitations so noted as my own caveats to success).

When it is working well, the results of teacher and administrative evaluation are fed back as a feedback loop system to the teacher or administrator to help them make improvements or corrections. If we find that a critical mass of our people are having difficulty in implementing an initiative, then changes need to be made in district plans, organizational structures, and professional development initiatives. Consequently, the personnel evaluation system is a critical component of the larger set of systems needed for school improvement.

Summary

School improvement can be understood in terms of an integrated systems approach incorporating all of the systems over which we have control. Once thought of as a linear approach, dealing with these systems as independent variables and organizing around those independent variables, school improvement efforts have sometimes been disappointing. But research and best practice in the private and public sectors have revealed that effective organizations are those in which the critical components are seen as integrated or interrelated in a larger system. Actions taken in subsystem A affect subsystem B in ways that are not always predictable and that may impact the overall goal and mission of the organization. Moreover, systems thinking and practice can only be carried out in an environment in which leadership and followers trust and respect one another.

The subsystems through which we conduct school improvement are program evaluation (or fast-track evaluation), planning, leadership and management, professional development, and personnel evaluation. Each of these systems has a methodology and science driving it, but they operate within the larger organization and in some relationship to the each of the other systems. It takes a special vision and ability to handle the stream of information coming from all directions to make sense of and effectively lead all of the activity within an organization toward an admirable goal. Data-driven decision-making is simply a toolset for a fast-track evaluation system. As Sergiovanni[125] noted, "the systems world provides the instrumental means, the management know-how, the operational systems, and the technical support that help us to achieve our goals, values, and dreams." There is a danger that the craft of data-driven decision-making will overtake the essential purpose of school improvement. Doing data-driven decision-making outside a larger context makes no more sense than evaluating teachers on criteria that are unrelated to the essence and nature of their craft. Thus, the goal is balance between organizational goals and culture and the tools to achieve them.

Notes

1. W. Cockel, Policy paper developed for the New England School Development Education Council, Marlborough, Mass., Spring 2000.

2. Peter Senge et al., *Schools That Learn: A Fifth Discipline Fieldbook for Educators, Parents, and Everyone Who Cares about Education* (New York: Doubleday Currency, 2000), 10.

3. Tom Peters, *Liberation Management: Necessary Disorganization for the Nanosecond Nineties* (New York: Alfred A. Knopf, 1992).

4. Jamshid Gharajedachi, *Systems Thinking: Managing Chaos and Complexity* (Boston, Mass.: Butterworth Heinemann, 1999), 15.

5. Joseph O'Connor and Ian McDermott, *The Art of Systems Thinking: Essential Skills for Creativity and Problem Solving* (San Francisco, Calif.: Thorsons, 1997).

6. Alan Kibbe Gaynor, *Analyzing Problems in Schools and School Systems: A Theoretical Approach* (Mahwah, N.J.: Lawrence Erlbaum Associates, Publishers, 1998).

7. Richard W. Scott, *Organizations: Rational, Natural, and Open Systems* (Upper Saddle River, N.J.: Prentice Hall, 1998).

8. Peter Senge et al., *The Fifth Discipline Fieldbook: Strategies and Tools for Building a Learning Organization* (New York: Doubleday Currency, 1994).

9. Gharajedaghi, *Systems Thinking*, 15.

10. Senge et al., *Schools That Learn*.

11. Bill Creech, *The Five Pillars of Total Quality Management: How to Make Total Quality Management Work for You* (New York: Truman Talley Books, 1995).

12. Bob Guns, *The Faster Learning Organization: Gain and Sustain the Competitive Edge* (San Diego, Calif.: Pfeiffer and Company, 1996).

13. Frances Hesslebein, Marshal Goldsmith, and Richard Beckhard, eds., *The Leader of the Future* (New York: Drucker Foundation, 1996).

14. Frances Hesslebein, Marshal Goldsmith, and Richard Beckhard, eds., *The Organization of the Future* (New York: Drucker Foundation, 1997).

15. Tom Peters, *The Circle of Innovation* (New York: Alfred A. Knopf, 1997).

16. Margaret J. Wheatley, *Leadership and the New Science: Learning about Organization from an Orderly Universe* (San Francisco, Calif.: Berret-Koehler Publishers, 1992).

17. Gharajedaghi, *Systems Thinking*, 15.

18. Gharajedaghi, *Systems Thinking*, 15–16.

19. Gharajedaghi, *Systems Thinking*, 8.

20. Wheatley, *Leadership and the New Science*.

21. Peters, *The Circle of Innovation* 273–275.

22. T. Sergiovanni, *The Lifeworld of Leadership* (San Francisco, Calif.: Jossey-Bass, 1999).

23. Senge et al., *Schools That Learn*.
24. Gharajedaghi, *Systems Thinking*.
25. O'Connor and McDermott, *The Art of Systems Thinking*.
26. Gaynor, *Analyzing Problems in Schools and School Systems*.
27. Scott, *Organizations*.
28. Senge et al., *The Fifth Discipline Fieldbook*.
29. Hesslebein, Goldsmith, and Beckhard, *The Leader of the Future*.
30. Peters, *The Circle of Innovation*.
31. Gaynor, *Analyzing Problems in Schools and School Systems*.
32. Senge et al., *The Fifth Discipline Fieldbook*.
33. O'Connor and McDermott, *The Art of Systems Thinking*.
34. Gharajedaghi, *Systems Thinking*.
35. O'Connor and McDermott, *The Art of Systems Thinking*.
36. Senge et al., *The Fifth Discipline Fieldbook*.
37. Senge et al., *Schools That Learn*.
38. Senge et al., *The Fifth Discipline Fieldbook*.
39. Peter Senge et al., *The Dance of Change: The Challenges to Sustaining Momentum in Learning Organizations* (New York: Doubleday Currency, 1999).
40. Senge et al., *Schools That Learn*.
41. Scott, *Organizations*.
42. Lee Bolman and Terrance Deal, *Reframing Organizations: Artistry, Choice, and Leadership*, second edition (San Francisco, Calif.: Jossey-Bass, 1997).
43. Sergiovanni, *The Lifeworld of Leadership*.
44. P. Streifer and C. Mojkowski, unpublished manuscript.
45. Gharajedaghi, *Systems Thinking*.
46. Ruth S. Johnson, *Setting Our Sights: Measuring Equity in School Change*. (Los Angeles, Calif.: Achievement Council, 1996.)
47. www.collegeboard.com, January 2000.
48. Creech, *The Five Pillars of Total Quality Management*.
49. Rafael Aguayo, *Dr. Deming: The American Who Taught the Japanese about Quality* (New York: Simon & Schuster, 1990).
50. Gharajedaghi, *Systems Thinking*, 27.
51. P. Everaert, "Emotions, Tempo, and Timing in Managing People," in *The Organization of the Future*, ed. Frances Hesslebein, Marshal Goldsmith, and Richard Beckhard (New York: Drucker Foundation, 1997), 275–286.
52. *Education Week*, "The Politics and Practice of Student Assessment," 2001. Found on the Web, March 2001. Web site: http://www.edweek.org.
53. *Education Week*, Special Report on "Quality Counts '99," 1999. Found on the Web, September 2000. Web site: http://www.edweek.org.
54. *Education Week*, Special Report on "Assessment," 1997. Found on the Web, October 26, 1997. Web site: http://www.edweek.org.
55. Rand, "The Use and Misuse of Test Scores in Reform Debate," 1994. Found on the Web, October 23, 1997. Web site: http://www.edweek.org.

56. Dennis P. Doyle and Susan Pimental, *Raising the Standard* (Thousand Oaks, Calif.: Corwin Press, 1997).

57. Peters, *The Circle of Innovation*, 318.

58. Senge et al., *The Fifth Discipline Fieldbook*.

59. Senge et al., *Schools That Learn*.

60. O'Connor and McDermott, *The Art of Systems Thinking*.

61. Senge et al., *Schools That Learn*.

62. Peters, *Liberation Management*.

63. Scott, *Organizations*.

64. Senge et al., *The Fifth Discipline Fieldbook*.

65. Creech, *The Five Pillars of Total Quality Management*.

66. Hesslebein, Goldsmith, and Beckhard, *The Leader of the Future*.

67. Peters, *The Circle of Innovation*.

68. Sergiovanni, *The Lifeworld of Leadership*.

69. Aguayo, *Dr. Deming*.

70. Arnold Weimerskirch and Stephen George, *Total Quality Management: Strategies and Techniques Proven at Today's Most Successful Companies* (New York: John Wiley & Sons, 1998).

71. James A. Belasco, *Teaching the Elephant to Dance: The Manager's Guide to Empowering Change* (New York: Plume, 1990).

72. Mike Schmoker, *Results: The Key to Continuous School Improvement* (Alexandria, Va.: Association for Supervision and Curriculum Development, 1996).

73. Peter M. Senge, *The Fifth Discipline: The Art & Practice of the Learning Organization* (New York: Doubleday Currency, 1990).

74. O'Connor and McDermott, *The Art of Systems Thinking*, 26.

75. Gharajedaghi, *Systems Thinking*.

76. Gharajedaghi, *Systems Thinking*.

77. William G. Cunningham and Gene R. Carter, *The American School Superintendent: Leading in an Age of Pressure* (San Francisco, Calif.: Jossey-Bass, 1997).

78. Senge et al., *Schools That Learn*, 7.

79. Gharajedaghi, *Systems Thinking*, 104–105.

80. Senge et al., *The Fifth Discipline Fieldbook*.

81. Stephen R. Covey, A. Roger Merrill, and Rebecca R. Merrill, *First Things First: To Live, to Love, to Learn, to Leave a Legacy* (New York: Simon & Schuster, 1996).

82. John W. Gardner, *On Leadership* (New York: Free Press, 1990).

83. Charles J. Schwahn and William G. Spady, *Total Leaders: Applying the Best Future-Focused Change Strategies to Education* (Arlington, Va.: American Association of School Administrators, 1998).

84. Peters, *The Circle of Innovation*, 142–143.

85. Peters, *The Circle of Innovation*.

86. Sergiovanni, *The Lifeworld of Leadership*, 4–8.

87. Cunningham and Carter, *The American School Superintendent*.

88. Susan Moore Johnson, *Leading to Change: The Challenge of the New Superintendency* (San Francisco, Calif.: Jossey-Bass, 1996).

89. John C. Maxwell, *The 21 Irrefutable Laws of Leadership* (Nashville, Tenn.: Thomas Nelson Publishers, 1998).

90. Creech, *The Five Pillars of Total Quality Management.*

91. Hesslebein, Goldsmith, and Beckhard, *The Leader of the Future.*

92. Wheatley, *Leadership and the New Science.*

93. Bolman and Deal, *Reframing Organizations.*

94. Belasco, *Teaching the Elephant to Dance.*

95. Covey, Merrill, and Merrill, *First Things First.*

96. Gardner, *On Leadership.*

97. Schwahn and Spady, *Total Leaders.*

98. Maxwell, *The 21 Irrefutable Laws of Leadership.*

99. J. A. Belasco and R. C. Stayer, *Flight of the Buffalo: Soaring to Excellence, Learning to Let Employees Lead* (New York: Warner Books, 1993).

100. Charles M. Farkas and Phillippe De Backer, *Maximum Leadership: Five Strategies for Success from the World's Leading CEOs* (New York: A Perigee Book, 1996).

101. Kenneth Leithwood and Roseanne Steinbach, *Expert Problem Solving: Evidence from School and District Leaders* (Albany: State University of New York Press, 1995).

102. Wess Roberts and Bill Ross, *Make It So: Leadership Lessons from Star Trek the Next Generation* (New York: Pocket Books, 1995).

103. C. Smith, *Computer-Supported Decision Making: Meeting the Decision Demands of Modern Organizations* (Greenwich, Conn.: Alex Publishing, 1998).

104. Penny Sebring and Anthony S. Bryk, "School Leadership and the Bottom Line in Chicago," *Phi Delta Kappan* 81, no. 6 (2000): 440–443.

105. Ken Blanchard, *The Heart of Leader* (Tulsa, Okla.: Honor Books, 1999).

106. Michael Fullen, *Leading in a Culture of Change* (New York: John Wiley & Sons, 2001).

107. Gardner, *On Leadership*, 24.

108. Sebring and Bryk, "School Leadership."

109. Hesslebein, Goldsmith, and Beckhard, *The Leader of the Future.*

110. Schwahn and Spady, *Total Leaders.*

111. Wheatley, *Leadership and the New Science.*

112. Cunningham and Carter, *The American School Superintendent.*

113. Johnson, *Leading to Change.*

114. Wheatley, *Leadership and the New Science*, 145.

115. Peters, *The Circle of Innovation*, 289.

116. Clearinghouse on Teaching and Teacher Education (1995), 1307 New York Ave., NW, Suite 300, Washington, D.C. 20005-4701.

117. Barry G. Sheckley and Morris T. Keeton, *Improving Employee Development: Perspectives from Research and Practice* (Chicago, Ill.: Council for Adult and Experiential Learning, 1997).

118. K. Killeen and D. Monk, "Local School District Spending on Professional Development: Insights Available from National Data," (paper presented at the NCES Summer Data Conference [1999 STATS-DC]), Washington, D.C., July 30, 1999.

119. The Interstate School Leaders Licensure Consortium, "Standards for School Leaders," by the Council of Chief State School Officers. Washington, D.C.: Author, 1996.

120. David Berliner, from a speech given at the Association for Supervision and Curriculum Development, 1988.

121. Jon Saphier and Robert Gower, *The Skillful Teacher: Building Your Teaching Skills* (Carlisle, Mass.: Research for Better Teaching, 1995).

122. Berliner, speech.

123. Banner and Cannon, *The Elements of Teaching* (New Haven, Conn.: Yale University Press, 1997).

124. *Evaluating Teaching: A Guide to Current Thinking and Best Practice*, edited by James Stronge (Thousand Oaks, Calif.; Corwin Press, 1997).

125. Thomas Sergiovanni, *The Lifeworld of Leadership: Creating Culture, Community, and Personal Meaning in Our Schools* (San Francisco, Calif.: Jossey-Bass, 2000), 180.

~

CHAPTER SEVEN

Data Extraction, Transformation, Analysis, and Graphing

Using more detailed data for decision-making than printed, "roll-up" or aggregate reports requires that these data be collected and analyzed. The process of collecting data and putting it into a database is known as extraction, transformation, and loading (ETL). This chapter discusses some of the issues and concerns in conducting this ETL process—a process that is necessary even if all we are doing is transforming test data into a spreadsheet for analysis. After ETL is completed, analysis can commence. Finally, data need to be properly displayed for interpretation and decision-making. This chapter also discusses some basic issues in data representation.

To facilitate the data-driven decision-making process, analyses should be performed electronically to maximize efficiency. For example, if we wanted to compare class grades with standardized test scores, it would be useful to place those data in a spreadsheet (or database) so that we could reanalyze them later or add more data for further analysis. Electronic data warehouses (discussed in chapter 8) are designed to provide easy access to all of these data. But what can you do without a data warehouse? Many chapters in this book discuss frames of analyses that can be conducted using basic tools such as "off the shelf" spreadsheets and database programs in lieu of a data warehouse.

As a starting point to achieve almost any level of serious analysis, data need to be brought (or imported) into a spreadsheet for processing. This is accomplished by either downloading them from a student information system or transforming "text" data received from a testing company and bringing (or importing) all of these data into one spreadsheet or database. To interpret the data, we know that a picture is worth a thousand words, which is why the graphical representation of data is so important for proper interpretation. This chapter will discuss basic techniques for data extraction from source diskettes, data clean up, recoding of variables to allow for proper analysis, adding data to files by hand, and then charting or graphing results for clarity.

Data Extraction Issues

The most overlooked problem in data-driven decision-making is getting the data into a format in which it can be processed. This is a critical issue that is normally left to database engineers, but one that must be considered and attended to even for basic analyses. Fortunately, there are some readily available "off the shelf" software tools for doing basic electronic data extraction and transformation that are useful if data, such as test scores, are received on a computer diskette. As a place to start, I would recommend that the district or school try to identify someone on staff who is familiar with these issues. Typically, one or more teachers will be familiar with simple database issues and can be very helpful. Some districts may be fortunate to have a database or management information system (MIS) specialist on staff who can perform this role. Certainly larger school districts will have a full MIS staff. But for smaller districts that do not have dedicated MIS staff, it will be important to find someone who can assist in this process. Another source of help could be students—many of whom no doubt will be skilled in these areas, but this raises concern over data confidentiality. These data contain detailed information about students and their performance in school or on standardized/mastery tests that is confidential and protected by federal law. Only authorized personnel should have access to these data. A strategy would be for students to train a member of the staff in data extraction and manipulation. Finally, it may be possible to hire a consultant to perform these data manipulations and transformations. It is not a lot of work and therefore should not be too costly. Regardless of how it gets done, data extraction and transformation are absolutely essential to moving forward and getting usable results.

The electronic data that are most useful for these analyses come from two main sources: testing (or state) agencies and downloads from one of the district's or school's operational systems such as the "student information system." When testing data are sent to districts or downloaded from the student information system, they are typically in ASCII format (sometimes DBF format as well). ASCII represents a standard format from which data can be transferred between and among different computer systems. For the general purposes outlined in this book, data should be requested in ASCII format. But occasionally data can be provided in DBF format, which is much easier to manipulate than ASCII. Many spreadsheet and database programs are able to read DBF format files directly and easily, including their field headers or field names—the importance of which will be made clear later—so if the data are available in this format, it would be a first choice. A last resort for those who do not want to deal with electronic data transformations is to enter all of the required data into a spreadsheet by hand. This gets the job done, but it is very cumbersome and time consuming. This is not recommended except as an absolute last resort.

Relational Databases

Depending on the skill of available staff, it would be most useful to put all of this data into a "relational database." Relational databases are database systems that can relate one dataset—test scores, for example—to another dataset that might include class grades. These data are linked in the system by a "key variable," which in most cases is the student ID assigned by the district. Similarly, a relational database could link a teacher demographic database to a professional development database through the key variable—"Teacher ID"— also assigned by the district. In more sophisticated systems, all of these data tables (and many others) can be linked. (Minimally, a data table is one set of data, such as a set of mastery tests from one year for a particular cohort of students. Data tables can become much more complex than this, but for our purposes here, we should try to keep data tables as simple as possible.) As the tables become more numerous and complex, a data warehouse will be needed to bring them all together. But basic "key" relationships can be built locally with inexpensive off the shelf database programs and skilled staff. An example of these data table relationships is shown in Figure 7.1.

When Do You Need Data Warehousing and What Can You Do Without It?

Data warehousing was developed for linking multiple data tables and even multiple databases for analysis. Beyond the simple example shown in Figure 7.1, this is highly complex work, and districts interested in this level of data table linking for analysis must consider acquiring one of these systems. As will be discussed in chapter 8, it is not practically possible for school staff to create a data warehouse, as they require highly complex data structures and "joins" (linking tables through student ID and teacher ID, for example).

Often the source data from the testing company or school student information system needs to be "reengineered" through a technique called field con-
catenation and other internal database manipulation, such as creating multiple primary keys, indexing, and setting primary/foreign key relationships to
make it all work in the data warehouse. If this sounds complex, it is. This author is familiar with several school districts that invested significant time and
resources in attempting to develop their own data warehouses and eventually
gave up due to the complexity involved. Those districts that have tried this
approach typically find themselves either with no system at all or with a system that few understand and is inflexible for future growth. Data warehousing "architecture" is both a science and an art—not to be attempted by un-
skilled practitioners.

However, at more simple levels such as those shown in Figure 7.1, district
personnel can begin developing their own simple databases. For example, many
of my students have conducted powerful data-driven decision-making exercises
relevant to their school settings using only a simple spreadsheet program. Some
have gone as far as creating a multiple table structure as shown in Figure 7.1. So

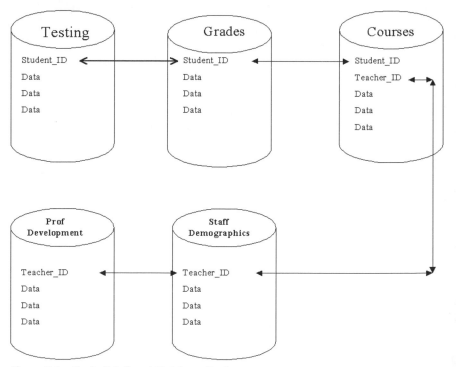

Figure 7.1 Basic Relational Database Design

don't be discouraged or frightened off—just be cautious with what you are attempting. My rules of thumb for deciding if you need a data warehouse are if you have to link data from more than two or three sources, or the "joins" are not apparent (such as every table having student ID)—then look at using a data warehouse. If the data you want to analyze do not all have student IDs, then look at using a data warehouse. And finally, if the data you want to analyze are dynamic, that is, they change often (even yearly such as standardized tests)—then look at using a data warehouse. But, if you simply want to do basic data disaggregation for a single data source or use data from a few tables that all have one common linking field, then go ahead and do this with a spreadsheet or a simple off the shelf database program.

If after following this advice you are at the stage of doing some analyses yourself, then the tools of choice for data transformation, manipulation, and analysis would be any one of the commonly available spreadsheet programs. These programs have several built-in routines designed to help handle basic data manipulation functions that anyone who is familiar with computers and simple database issues can learn. Moreover, some of the spreadsheet programs have easy-to-use and powerful statistics for performing the analyses needed to draw meaning from the data. Thus, in one easy-to-use tool we can have all the building blocks to perform fairly sophisticated data-driven decision-making processes.

Data Extraction and Import—Transforming and Loading ASCII Data into a Spreadsheet

Once the data needed for analysis have been identified, they must be placed into a spreadsheet for analyses. This section will provide a description of how to move ASCII data into a spreadsheet program.

Let's assume that we have received either state mastery test data or some other standardized testing data for a particular group of students, and we want to run a basic correlation between language subscores. The process of readying the data for analysis requires that we first import them into a spreadsheet program and then clean up any data fields that contain spurious entries, such as missing values for students absent for one or more tests.

Importing the Data to a Spreadsheet or Database

To import these data into a spreadsheet or database program, use the diskette sent by the testing company that typically contains the data in ASCII format. Many spreadsheet and database programs have a text import wizard that will help you easily import the raw text or ASCII data. When you go to import these data with the text import wizard, these programs will ask you whether the data are "Delimited" or "Fixed Width." ASCII (or text files) contains all of the data separated by a character such as a comma or tab, or the data may be in fixed-width columns/fields. *Delimited* means separated by, for example, commas, tabs, spaces, and so on. *Fixed width* means that the data are in some predetermined "fixed" width that must be separated manually—using the program—based on a structure provided by the vendor of the data. Fixed-width fields do not imply that all the fields will be a certain width either. Typically, fixed-width fields within any given dataset can vary widely.

For example, if the data file only had two columns or fields, such as "last name" and "first name," we would have to tell the spreadsheet or database program how these columns or fields are separated in the source file (the file as it was received from the testing company). Most of the time, the data will be separated or delimited with a character such as a comma or tab. Thus, in order to extract the data from the source file, we need to specify how the data fields are separated. There will be a screen asking you if field names are in the first row; if you know that they are, check this box. Doing so will set up each spreadsheet or data table field/column with its field header or name. If the source data does not contain field names in the first row (often the case) you will need to add them manually once the data are imported. If the data are delimited, in most cases you can now check "Finish," and the program will automatically put the data into a spreadsheet (or data table if you are using a database program).

There are other cases, discussed next, in which the data might be organized into fixed-width (or length) fields—for example, nine characters in one field, three in another, then a series of ten fields all two characters long. If this were the case then we would check "Fixed Width" in the text import wizard.

If the data are fixed width we must tell the program what those specific field lengths are, specifying what fields should be imported and giving each field a name. This is a more complex process than if the data were delimited, and you will need to follow the spreadsheet or database program directions carefully. You will also need a codebook, described later, to determine what field(s) represent what data.

If most of your data are fixed width, be cautioned that this will be a laborious and time-consuming task. If all you need to do is process one dataset, then go ahead—the work will be worth it. But if you have several datasets to process, you should look to more sophisticated programs that allow you to save these import routines once created. For example, let's say that you have a student testing dataset from fourth grade, year 2000, that has 150 fields in fixed width of various lengths. It would take you a couple of hours to set up the import routine for a spreadsheet or database program to import these data properly. If that is all you were going to process, the work would probably be worth it. But then suppose you had fourth grade from 1999 and 1998, all of which have the same data structure as the 2000 dataset, and you wanted to import all of these data as well to do a longitu-dinal study. You would have to go through that laborious two-hour process for each of these additional datasets, as most spreadsheet and database pro-grams do not allow you to store or save the import routine created for the first dataset. There are, however, programs that do allow you to save these routines, although they are a good deal more expensive. In the end, you will have to weigh the cost of someone's time to keep going through these text import processes as opposed to purchasing one of the more powerful pro-grams that can store these routines. Most of the more sophisticated statisti-cal programs have this feature. There are also some shareware programs that purport to allow you to save these routines.

When you import fixed-width data using the text wizard, you have con-trol of where to separate the fields, according to the structure provided by the vendor. This typically entails moving vertical lines in and out of the data at specified places in the dataset. So if the dataset had a total of 1,000 charac-ters, spaces 1 to 4, for example, might contain "year," spaces 5 to 20 "first name," 21 to 35 "last name," and so on.

In some of these datasets, an entire string of scores are located together. For example, if we were looking at reading scores, we might find a string such as this: 8865075 in spaces 30 to 36. This string might reflect three separate scores for a student's reading test. The first two digits, 88, might be national percentile; the middle three digits could be scale score; and the final two dig-its might be NCE score. Upon import we would need to make each score a separate field for analysis in the spreadsheet, and to accomplish this, we would add those vertical lines, or field separators as follows: 88 | 650 | 75. This requires a lot of work and a codebook from the testing company/vendor to understand what scores are in what columns. The codebook might read: Reading National Percentile—Columns 30–31; Reading Scale Scores—Columns 32–34; Reading NCE—Columns 35–36; and the like. Using this information and the text import wizard, we could separate the columns as needed.

If you make a mistake throughout this process (not too difficult to do, I might add), some spreadsheet programs have functions that allow you to go back and further break columns of data into new fields (these functions are sometimes called "text to data" functions). But these functions are beyond the scope of this book. It's important to realize that this is a complex, and sometimes boring, process but a very necessary one to get the data into the spreadsheet for analysis.

At this point, once we are satisfied that the data are in proper columns, or fields, we can press "Finish" to complete the import process that loads the data into the spreadsheet format (or database table). The data are now ready for processing, assuming there are no serious data clean-up issues.

Data Clean-Up

When data are imported into a spreadsheet or database program from a source such as a standardized testing file, two problems often need to be addressed or "cleaned up" before any processing can begin. Imported data typically have either "missing values" coded for students who did not get a score for some reason and "dirty," or spurious, data entries. Missing values occur when the testing company inputs a special value for students who were absent from the test or subtest. Typical values used are "99," "998," and "999." We can eliminate these missing values using the "Find/Replace" function in most spreadsheet programs. Similar problems such as dirty data can occur, for example, when a field has something like "#EMPTY" instead of a blank field with no value or a zero. All of these problems need to be cleaned up prior to analysis, as they will either cause the program to crash (as you are trying to process nonnumeric data) or they will seriously skew the results (trying to average scores with a range of 1 to 130, including missing values such as 998).

To clean up dirty data or to clean out missing values, use the "Find/Replace" function included in all of these programs. You do this by highlighting the field with the bad data and then going to the "Find/Replace" function. Enter the values you want to find, and then replace them with the substitute (sometimes a blank—see below), finishing the process by selecting "Replace All." The program will replace all the bad data with the values you entered in the "Replace With" box.

In the example above, let's say a dataset had several fields loaded with "#EMPTY" instead of a blank field with no value or a zero. The task is to clean out the "#EMPTY," leaving no value whatsoever because no value in a field is better for some statistical functions to follow. To clean this up, enter "#EMPTY" into the "Find" box and DO NOT ENTER ANYTHING in the "Replace" box—in other words, leave the replace box empty—don't even place a space in it, as spaces are interpreted by statistics programs as text data. By pressing "Replace All," the program will automatically replace "#EMPTY" with nothing, leaving the column or field of data ready for analysis. You can do this for multiple columns or fields at once with many of these programs, saving time and keystrokes.

If we wanted to replace the text "male" with the value "2," we would place "male" in the "Find What" box and "2" in the "Replace With" box. The reason for doing so will be discussed later in the recode section. Once you have completed all the replacements necessary, the data in the file are now ready for analysis, but be sure to save your work before exiting the program!

Recoding Data for Better Analyses and Interpretation

Sometimes when we import data for analysis, letters are coded instead of numbers in fields or variables. If, for example, we want to determine the difference in performance between girls and boys and gender is coded "F" for female and "M" for male, we would have to change these letters to numbers to do the analysis. (If you are using a high-end statistics program, this is not necessary, as these programs can read and process text like "M" as an independent variable.) This process is called "recoding the data." To run statistics in most programs you would need to replace these letters or names (text data) with numeric values such as "1" or "2," recoding, for example, "Female" as "1" and "Male" as "2."

To replace "Female" with "1," follow the same steps as in cleaning up the data: choose the "Find/Replace" function from the "Edit" menu, only in this case we will insert a value of "1" for "Replace With." After highlighting the data and selecting the functions, enter "Female" into the "Find What" box and "1" into the "Replace With" box—then press "Replace All." Doing so will replace the word "Female" with the number "1" anywhere in the highlighted data that we are working on. Repeat this process replacing the word "Male" with "2." This now results in a file ready for processing because the titles "Female" and "Male" have been changed to values that the program can recognize and use in running basic statistics.

What would have happened had we reversed the process, that is, replace "Male" before "Female"? Since "male" is part of the word "female," the computer would have replaced the "female" fields with the following: "Fe2." This would not be catastrophic as we could simply ask the system to subsequently replace "Fe2" with "1." But it's startling sometimes to see the unexpected; thus, it's important to follow these steps logically.

Text and Numeric Field Types

Spreadsheet and database programs use a large number of field types, two of which we are dealing with here. Data that is in text format, such as "male" or "female," are referred to as text data. Numbers, such as "1" and "2," are referred to as numeric data. Several other types of fields are beyond the scope of this discussion, such as various date types, time, integer, currency, and percentage. When data are first imported into a spreadsheet or database program, as discussed earlier in this chapter, the program reads the data type of the source data and automatically sets that data type for the field. So if we had imported text data such as "male" and "female," the program would have set the data type to text. However, if we then transform these data into the numbers "1" and "2," the program would not automatically recognize this change. The program would simply interpret "1" and "2" as text data. We need to tell the program that we want the field type changed to numeric. This is accomplished in many programs through a field formatting procedure. In some spreadsheet programs, you can highlight the field and right click with the mouse to find the formatting function. But you will probably have to read the manual to find out how to do this.

You need to change the field type to analyze the data. Keeping with our example from before, let's say you wanted to determine the difference between male and female scores. To do this you would want to use a t-test. However, in most of these programs, the t-test function cannot recognize text data. So if you did not change these text data to numeric format, the program would crash when you tried to run the t-test using "1" and "2" held in a text field as read by the program.

To sum up, processing data for analysis requires three basic steps. First, the data must be transformed from its source disk into a spreadsheet or database. Next, it has to be cleaned and recoded if necessary. Finally, you must be sure to set the field format properly, typically changing text for numeric format. If this sounds complex, it is. As you begin to process more and more data of different data types, the complexity grows. Data warehousing specialists handle all of this work for you when they build a data warehouse.

Adding Data to the Spreadsheet File

At times we may want to add data to an existing file. For example, if we want to determine the relationship between student class grades and the results of those students on a standardized test, we have to add the class grades to the file containing the test scores. Sophisticated methods can combine these data if we have the class grades in an ASCII format and coded by student ID and if we have someone on staff who has skill with one of the relational data-base programs. However, for most of us who do not possess these skills, there is a more straightforward method of solving this problem—although it is more labor intensive. We can simply type in the desired data in a new field that we create in the spreadsheet file. Practically speaking, this method works if we have limited research questions, a small number of data fields to enter, and limited numbers of students to deal with. However, if the number of students you are dealing with exceeds these parameters, then you will probably be better off in the long run using a database program to combine these data. Because of the sheer amount of work involved, the investment you make in finding someone who can perform the database functions will be worth your while.

To add student grades in math to a file that contains math scores from a standardized test, follow these steps.

1. Select the test score file you want, and bring it into your spreadsheet program if it has not already been imported as described above in the section "Importing the Data." Select the grades you want to add, and compile a list by student and grade. This information should be avail-able from the school grading system as a computer printout. You should also be able to get a listing that you can sort alphabetically by class.

2. In small files, that is, files with just ten or fifteen students, it is easy to find each student's name, but in larger files, it will be helpful to sort by last name to create an alphabetical list that we can use to match up with the class grades printout. To sort the file, first select all the data in the file following the directions of your spreadsheet program. Many of these programs allow you to sort the entire dataset by placing the cursor in cell A1 and then selecting "Data" on the main tool bar and then "Sort."

3. This brings you to a dialogue box that asks what field or variable you want to sort on. It will be pointing to the first column in your dataset that may or may not be student name—the field that is needed to cre-ate an alphabetical listing by student. If the program is not indicating it will sort on student name, change the sort functions as needed. Most of these programs allow you to perform secondary sorts, for example, sorting on first name after last name. This will be useful when working with larger files. Now that we have the data in alphabetical order by last name, we need to add the student math grades retrieved from the school grading system that is probably on a list or printout.

4. Add a column in the spreadsheet for the new data to be added. Do this by selecting "Insert" and "Columns" from the main tool bar of your spreadsheet program. The result is a new blank column for the data that we are about to add.
5. Now, type in the field name of the data in the first cell of the column, such as "Math Grades."
6. Finally, type in the new data for each student in the blank column just added. If the class grades are represented by letters such as B+, A-, C, and so on, you should transform these letter grades to numbers before putting them into the spreadsheet program or you will need to "Replace" these values later and change the field format.

This concludes the sections on importing, cleaning, recoding, and adding data. By following these procedures you will be able to perform important analyses on your data, including testing for group differences and group relationships and setting performance targets. While these data extraction, cleaning, recoding, and adding data procedures may appear complex, with a little time and practice they can provide you with a powerful ability to manipulate small datasets so they can be processed for decision-making.

Graphing for Clarity of Decision-Making

It is said that a picture is worth a thousand words, and this is certainly the case when trying to interpret educational data for decision-making. Educators are awash in so much data—commonly in the form of charts and printouts for test reports, class grades, attendance records, dropout rates, and the like—that it is often difficult to interpret all of these data and to act. Moreover, it is possible to misinterpret data due to the confusion of having so much of it before us. Clarity is needed to assist decision-makers in sorting through all of this and making sense of it all.

However, charting or graphing the data may not be sufficient for clarity unless it is done with care and expertise. Edward Tufte[1] provides one of the best explanations for why proper graph construction is needed for effective decision-making. In his book *Visual Explanations: Images and Quantities, Evidence and Narrative*, he describes several examples of human catastrophes or otherwise unexplainable events that could have been better understood if a properly drawn visual representation had been constructed. For example, he notes that had London officials plotted incidences of cholera during the outbreak of 1854, they would have easily determined the cause.

A more recent and dramatic example is the space shuttle *Challenger* disaster of 1986. As in so many national tragedies, many of us can remember exactly what we were doing when we heard that the *Challenger* had exploded shortly after liftoff on that cold January day in 1986. Tufte's explanation of how properly constructed charts might have prevented the tragedy is compelling.

Tufte analyzed the data that NASA and the White House reviewed that morning prior to authorizing the launch. The data include several instances where there had been O-ring blow-by in previous launches. The reader will remember that when the shuttle takes off, it is provided a boost by the solid fuel strap-on booster rockets that are discarded later in the flight and returned to earth for re-use. In previous launches, there had been O-ring blow-by (a condition where the solid fuel leaks out through defective or misaligned O-rings that are used to seal joints on the booster rockets, shielding the large center fuel tank from any hot gases or flames). These previous problems were presented to NASA prior to the *Challenger* launch in what Tufte termed "chart junk." This was because the data were sorted by launch date—not temperature, which was the critically important variable that cold January morning in Florida. Viewing the data by launch date does not reveal the relationship between low temperatures and O-ring blow-by in previous launches. Moreover, Tufte argues, that had the data been displayed on a chart where the scale of the temperature variable took into consideration the unusually cold morning that day, the case to scrub the launch would have been even more compelling.

Many questions have been left unanswered about the decision to launch the *Challenger* that morning as several Morton Thiokol engineers (Morton Thiokol makes the booster rockets) resigned in protest after their warnings of an impending disaster went unheeded. Whether their warnings, in conjunction with a properly constructed visual representation of the problem, would have been sufficient to stave off this disaster will never be known. What does become clear from Tufte's work is that a properly drawn chart of a problem can be clarifying and helpful in making decisions from otherwise difficult to understand data.

In a simple experiment, I applied these ideas to help school personnel make a decision. The problem was how to allocate approximately $5,000 for curriculum development around a strategic goal of improving student achievement on state mastery test performance. School personnel were asked to review all the data they had at hand and to make a decision and support their findings. After several meetings, the committee could not come to a satisfactory solution. I then presented two sets of data in basic charts to help them decide whether the dollars should be allocated for reading or mathematics curriculum/professional development work. The charts are shown in Figures 7.2 and 7.3.

Both sets of charts display the same data variables, but one is for reading and the other for math. Figure 7.2 shows the reading scores from the Connecticut Mastery Test (DRP scores) for eighth-grade students and these same students' verbal ability scores (VANCE) from a different test, the Comprehensive Testing Program (CTPIII, published by the Educational Records Bureau). The comparative data is presented in Figure 7.3, displaying these students' math raw scores on the Connecticut Mastery Test and their quantitative ability scores (QANCE) on the CTPIII. Overlaying each chart is the standard curve, that is, what would normally be expected given this distribution of students. Comparing these two sets of data in chart format, I asked the team to decide where to allocate their $5,000 and to support their decision. After previously sifting through reams of data that were now presented with a clear representation of the critically important variables, the team was able to come to a determination within minutes. While the data presented in Figure 7.3 show a close correspondence between achievement and ability for math, the same is not true for reading. There is a group of stu-

Data Presentation for Analysis and Decision-Making

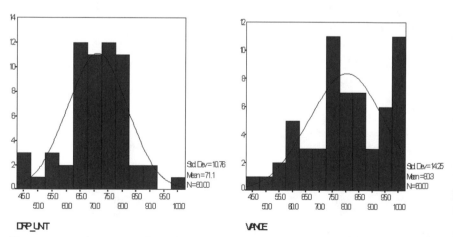

Figure 7.2   Histograms of Reading Achievement and Verbal Ability Scores for the Same Students

Data Presentation for Analysis and Decision-Making

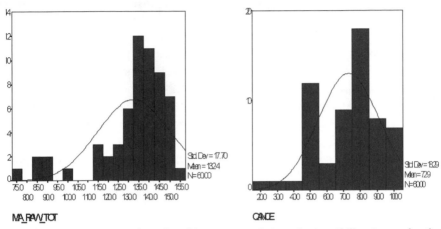

Figure 7.3 Histograms of Math Achievement and Quantitative Ability Scores for the Same Students

dents whose reading achievement is below that of their verbal ability (the group skewed to the right of the VANCE chart). Since both tests are reasonably valid and reliable measures and because these are the data that we had available to make this decision, it was possible to conclude quickly that reading is the place to allocate the funds.

I recognize that many educators would argue against comparing reading and math achievement using verbal and quantitative ability measures due to the inherent problems with student ability data. However, the same could be said for the achievement data. There will always be problems with the appropriateness, reliability, and validity of these data that could be used to argue against making these comparisons. In a fast-track decision-making/evaluation mode, as described in previous chapters, educators are called upon to make these decisions daily, with or without the data, and all too often without. Or, as in this case, we find ourselves pouring over reams of data, taking up too much of our valuable time without coming to a reasonable conclusion. The point here is that, while these data may be somewhat flawed, we must also recognize that real decisions need to be made every day in schools on even less solid evidence. It is the opinion of this author that those decisions should be data-driven to the greatest extent possible, recognizing the limits inherent in the data used to make those decisions.

Creating Graphs for Decision-Making

How can we easily and quickly create charts/graphs that can be used for decision-making? How can we draw the standard curve over our data to help in that decision-making? The answer lies in powerful yet inexpensive, recently available software. There are several statistical programs and spreadsheet programs that allow you to easily graph data for visual presentation and decision-making. Some of these programs allow you to overlay the normal curve such as that shown in Figures 7.2 and 7.3. Some spreadsheet programs have excellent graphing capability (minus the ability to overlay the normal curve), and they have easy-to-use statistical functions built in, such as correlation, histogram, ANOVA, and t-test. (As a general rule, if you need to run more sophisticated statistics than these, such as ANOVA, ANCOVA, or regression, you should consider one of the high-end statistics programs.) The issue of what computer program to use comes down to your own facility in using these programs and the time you can allocate to the learning curve. If your ability is limited and you do not have the time to learn more than one program, stay with a basic spreadsheet program for the graphing and basic statistics functions since you will almost always want to start with a spreadsheet for data manipulation, clean-up, recoding, and other transformations.

Summary

This chapter covered the critical issues in data-driven decision-making: how to manipulate the data, readying them for analysis, and using graphing for better representations of the data for improved decision-making. It has been said that there is nothing pretty about data extraction, transformation, and loading (into the spreadsheet or database)—a truism in this work. But all too often this step is overlooked, either in terms of its importance for making sure that only "clean" and "usable" data are analyzed or for its sheer drudgery. But the final inferences we draw from the data and decisions we make are completely dependent on these steps. Finally, we have learned that it is possible to go through all these steps and do the proper analyses only to misinterpret the data because they were not represented properly or clearly. Paying attention to these steps, one at the beginning, the other at the end of the data-driven decision-making process, will help ensure that the best possible decisions are made.

Note

1. Edward R. Tufte, *Visual Explanations: Images and Quantities, Evidence and Narrative.* Cheshire, Conn.: Graphics Press, 1997.

~

CHAPTER EIGHT

The Emerging Role of Information Technologies: Making Better Decisions through Knowledge Density

Educational decision-making is standing on the threshold of major advancements with the expanded use of information technologies. Of the advancements made in the private sector over the past decade, two stand out that hold great promise for the improvement of educational decision-making: (1) the management of thousands of disparate data elements across multiple years of data accumulation and (2) multidimensional problem-solving techniques that now become possible through use of advanced informational technologies that help us access and analyze data. Most recently the technologies to accomplish all of this have come down in price and that trend continues.

As the various data we have to analyze becomes richer by virtue of the number of variables we can access across multiple cohorts and years, our database could be said to become more "dense." When we use decision support tools to explore that richly expanded database, our knowledge about the problems under review also becomes enriched or enhanced. I term this richness and improvement in our knowledge about the problem "knowledge density," a term borrowed from the information technology sector.[1] This chapter explores how improved knowledge density can lead to improved decision-making about important student improvement problems.

What Will the Data-Driven Decision-Making Process Look Like in This New Environment?

Regardless of how we conduct data-driven decision-making (by hand or with high-tech computerized decision-support tools), some overarching concepts apply to the process. Most important of these is the data-driven decision-making process itself that proceeds from inquiry to analysis, followed by decision-making as discussed in chapter 1. The questions we raise will range from simple to complex, often emanating from a review of student outcome measures such as test results. Or they may result from a hypothesis derived mostly from our observations, coupled perhaps with quantitative data analysis, such as a review of the number of girls taking advanced math courses over a concern for gender equity. As we review these data, we pose questions that formulate our inquiries. How many girls take advanced math courses? How do they perform in those classes? What courses do most girls take? What is their level of preparation compared with the boys'? Do boys and girls do equally well on rigorous standardized tests? If not, where are the differences? What are guidance counselors saying to girls about math careers? What are the prerequisites for a rigorous high school math track? Must students take algebra in eighth grade? If so, what are the prerequisites for that course? And so on.

We have learned that how these inquires are framed is important to the overall success of the decision-making process.[2] Then, once the problem is framed into its subsets, appropriate data need to be collected and analyzed. Current methods of data collection and analysis used by schools are labor intensive, but even with new emerging technologies, attention must be paid to issues such as data integrity and the use of proper measurement scales and appropriate statistics.

In addition to framing the problem properly, we also know that our level of thinking about problems becomes more multidimensional in an information technology (IT) environment.[3-5] This ability to manage more data elements through IT not only improves efficiency but also directly affects the quality of the inquiry process itself. This is what I mean by knowledge density, or the ability to know more deeply about a problem based on the range and depth of the data we have available for analysis. Using paper and pencil data-driven decision-making methods, we know that knowledge density is limited and that the resulting decisions are thus likely to have limited impact. In this sense, the quality of our decisions and the potential for them to affect improvement is linked to the depth and robustness of our data, coupled with our ability to analyze that data over multiple dimensions. Integral to this interplay between inquiry and the analysis of data is the benchmarking process. Ultimately, improvement is realized through actions that move a program from "what is" to "what should be." Deciding what should be is a benchmarking issue—to both internal *and* external standards (but as we saw in chapter 6, one must be careful not to benchmark too low, as this process is an artful mix of science and intuition about what is possible and how far the organization can be stretched without losing confidence in its leadership). In the final analysis, the more data we have, the more knowledge density we have, and when coupled with the use of proper analytical techniques and appropriate statistics, better decisions are likely to result.

The Role of Wisdom and Experience
Driven by Knowledge Density

In every field of endeavor, there is just no substitute for experience and wisdom in the decision-making process. However, the benefits of experience can be severely limited when knowledge density is low. No decision is factless, but many educational decisions today are made on scant data analysis, limited by the availability and access to those data. This has led, in my opinion, to a lack of creativity and innovation in the decision-making process, at least as compared with what is possible in a data warehousing environment.

The decision-making process is highly dependent on knowledge density, driving the reformulation or reframing of problems supported through the proper analysis of reliable and valid data. In complex social organizations such as schools, the best decisions are those that rely both on qualitative data gathered through observation and analyses of related quantitative data. Hirshberg,[6] founder and president of Nissan Design International, speaks to this special relationship between intuition and data when he says, "Creativity is the mastery of information and skills in the service of dreams." Hirshberg refers to this as "informed intuition," especially as it applies to creativity in the decision-making process.

> Well-developed intuitive skills require well-deployed antennae, considerable experience, and as much practice at *intellectually feeling* the tone and potential of a complex whole as skilled logical analysis and the use of the scientific method. And intuition demands the open sharing of undoctored information and considerable encouragement from executives long associated with cool, objective thinking. (211–212)

Hirshberg's description is particularly useful because our goal should be the attainment of high-quality decisions based on wisdom and experience informed by "skilled logical analysis and the use of the scientific method," as he puts it. As discussed in chapter 6, we need innovation and creativity to solve tough educational problems. It is clear that the deeper answers, if they exist, lie in our ability to conduct data analyses with as much precision as possible, coupled with our intuition that is developed over years of experience dealing with problems in the field.

When Does Data Become Information?

Data alone tell us nothing. As we bring data together to be analyzed, we *may* derive information—but not necessarily. For example, knowing that more students are enrolled in higher-level math classes by itself is an interesting fact, but we don't know if it is due to larger enrollments overall or if there are more girls enrolled now than in previous years, a reasonable question if we are concerned about gender equity. Similarly, knowing that tenth-grade mastery test scores are down by itself does not tell us nearly as much as determining how students did who were enrolled in the school over a three-year time period as compared with students from either an earlier cohort or those who entered the school within the past two years. In all cases, information is derived from basic data by virtue of asking the right question and conducting the appropriate analysis. Thus, as information is improved through the analyses of data, knowledge density increases. However, knowledge density is not just an analogy for information. Knowledge density is also affected by the quality of the various queries and the correctness of the analyses, as the following section explains.

Using the Data Cube Representation of Data for Planning Trend Analyses

We can start with the data cube as an aid in thinking about inquiry, analysis, and knowledge density. The data cube, as used in the information technology sector,[7-9] helps conceptualize both the concept map and the interplay among data elements and multidimensional thinking, that is, analyses over time and many variables. At any level of knowledge density, it is useful to represent the problem using the data cube to aid in the data-driven decision-making process. (It's important to note that the data cube has other applications in IT, particularly as a subset of data from the data warehouse. That application is acknowledged but not used here. In the context used here, the data cube helps represent the data selected to address the problem at hand.)

Consider the SAT example discussed in earlier chapters. Our high school has just learned that its Scholastic Achievement Test (SAT) scores for the class of 1998 dropped by 48 points (23 in math and 25 in verbal). The administration wants to act quickly to determine what caused the downward turn and to determine what can be done to prevent a recurrence. In working through the initial inquiry process, a number of questions come to mind:

1. How did the class of 1998 do on its PSAT exams and on other standardized tests in middle and high school?
2. What courses did the class of 1998 take?
3. How did the class of 1998 do in school as evidenced by class grades?
4. What percentage of the class of 1998 is new to the school within the past three years?
5. What percentage of the class of 1998 works, and for how many hours per week?

The visual representation of these questions can be displayed on a simple data cube with each vertical and horizontal bar (or row/column) being a potential analysis. Adding to the complexity, we can conceptualize questions between and among rows and columns, such as the relationship of test scores to course-taking trends over a three-year period (see Figure 2.8 in chapter 2).

All of these questions are important to understanding what happened to the SAT scores, but they are limited (i.e., they cover data that apply to this class only over time). We can expand the dimensions by asking questions 6–10:

6. Was this an anomaly, or have previous classes had lower performance?
7. How did other cohorts (the classes of 1997 and 1996) do on these tests?
8. What courses and grades did other cohorts take and receive as compared with their SAT scores?
9. What was the percentage of students in other classes who worked, and for how long each week?
10. What is the interrelationship among variables between these three classes, and how do these interactions relate to SAT scores?

A more complex hypercube emerges when we consider these new dimensions, as shown in Figure 2.9 in chapter 2. As the data cube representation becomes more complex, no doubt knowledge density increases, but so does the complexity of the data analyses. We can also see that the initial query becomes expanded from "Why did the class of 1998's SAT scores go down?" to questions about the interplay among the ten questions discussed above and the SAT score decline. Simply asking why the SAT scores are down followed by the review of limited data (assuming we are doing all this by hand) is not likely to yield a robust understanding about how the school should go forward in correcting the problem. Conducting analyses among the broader array of data in the more complex data cube (Figure 2.9) is much more likely to yield a wider range of possible decision points and potential actions.

Decision-making in corporate settings long ago reached the point where simple analyses could no longer provide adequate information for decision-making.[10] To analyze more and more complex issues, special technologies emerged, such as data warehousing and data repositories.[11–15] Data warehousing and information management systems have been in widespread use in the private sector for a decade or more, but they are just now becoming available (and affordable) for educational use.[16,17] Even more elaborate technologies based on complex algorithms derived from the many potential relationships of data elements (within the data cube) now assist private-sector decision-makers, as well as various governmental functions[18,19] in the name of rule-based and case-based decision-making techniques.

How complex can all of this become? Consider that the National Center for Educational Statistics has developed a coding system for literally every data element potentially in use in modern school districts. These now total over 4,500 separate data elements. Data warehouses and data repositories have been developed that can load and access all of these data elements, and more, over a thirteen-year or more period—all on one computer screen. This creates an initial cube of 4500 × 13 (Figure 8.1) with literally millions of potential relationships between and among these data elements (thirteen years

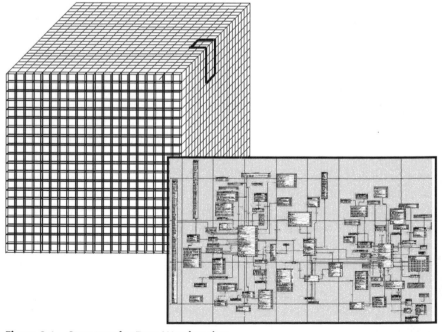

Figure 8.1   Structure for Data Warehousing

represent the vertical axis with the 4,500 elements comprising both the Y-and X-axes). In fact, there are so many potential relationships that we cannot possibly conceive of them all. This same problem led to the creation of special technologies, called "data mining programs," used to identify potential relationships among the data elements.[20-22] Some of these tools are complex and expensive, but the basic technology is not out of the reach of educators.

A cube of 4500 × 13, a three-dimensional matrix covering 4,500 data elements each over thirteen years, yields either high knowledge density or incredible confusion. Trying to manipulate the data within this cube using typical data-driven decision-making methods (paper and pencil) is like trying to compute by hand the propulsion needs and trajectory of a rocket to Mars. Chances are we wouldn't do it. Now, going to Mars is simply not possible without making the computations (let alone the technology) to get us there! So in the absence of high-speed computers and fancy celestial mechanics and propulsion software programs, if we were determined to go to Mars (now being seriously contemplated[23]), we would have to do the computations by hand! Working through all of this complexity, we would likely make mistakes or worse—take short cuts. If we labored hard to get the final solutions but subsequently found some errors in the computations, we might be willing to chance a launch in the face of a closing launch window (as Mars comes into close proximity of Earth once every few years). Unfortunately, doing so could lead to catastrophe. We might also be so invested in our analyses that we would fail to see our error. Either way, the chances of everything going just right diminish as knowledge density and analytical accuracy declines. In this example, poor data, limited data, and/or poor data analyses can cause low knowledge density. And clearly, the risk goes up when decisions are based on limited data and/or poor analysis. So, do we launch? Probably not. Yet every day these same conditions apply to the countless decisions being made in our schools. Thus, our goal should be to maximize knowledge density, thereby ensuring that the decisions we make have a high potential for success and to limit those decisions based on intuition alone or low knowledge density.

Putting All of This to Use

Inputs, Processes, and Outcomes

How can we make sense and use of all these data? The data elements within the 4500 x13 cube can be thought of as falling into one of three categories: inputs, processes, or outcome variables (see Figure 8.2). These relationships will also help drive our inquiries and help frame solutions. Input variables include such things as student ability and demographics. Process variables

Thinking About Data and Improvement

Input Variables   Outcomes

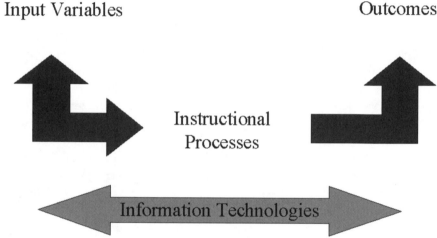

Instructional
Processes

Information Technologies

Figure 8.2   Categories of Data for School Improvement Analyses

include those that describe what is done to improve achievement—from re-source allocation to staff development to using new instructional materials and techniques. Outcome measures include test scores and class grades. Student course-taking trends can be either input or output variables. In the SAT example cited earlier, course-taking trends were input variables as we looked to identify trends that might explain a drop of 28 points in the class of 1998's scores. They can also be outcome variables such as in the gender bias issue discussed earlier, when we disaggregated student enrollment in upper-level math courses to understand who was enrolling. As these relationships become more and more complex, or more multidimensional, it is useful to frame problems and the data needed to analyze those problems in this model.

What Are Data Warehousing and Information Management Systems?

School and district data initially reside in operational systems that often do not allow for easy query of those data. For example, student absenteeism, discipline, and demographics are held within a student management system. Course schedules and grades are handled within another component of that same student management system, but often it is difficult to manage data elements across and among all of these components, even if they are in the "same system." One Connecticut district that had spent a large sum of money on a new student information system found that it could not isolate and disaggregate student class grades by such factors as discipline referrals or absenteeism, even though all of these data resided in the same computer system, without ordering an expensive custom report from the vendor. Also, standardized test results (separate unto themselves), budget data, and personnel systems are not typically linked together but are all in separate systems as well. Consequently, we are left with a number of disparate operational computer systems that perform their intended functions well but are inflexible when it comes to comparing and analyzing data across these systems (that is, you cannot take data from one system and analyze it with data from another system). This problem is shown in Figure 8.3.

These very same problems existed in the private sector, that of linking disparate data across separate operational systems, which led to the development

Challenge–Bring all Data Together

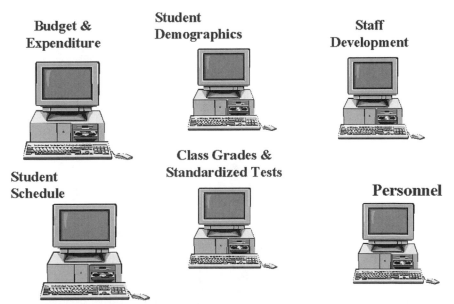

Budget & Expenditure

Student Demographics

Staff Development

Student Schedule

Class Grades & Standardized Tests

Personnel

Figure 8.3   The Need for Data Extraction, Transformation, and Loading into the Data Warehouse

of "data warehouses," or large data repositories into which all of the data from each of these operational systems is dumped.[24,25] Using highly sophisticated relational databases, data warehouses link all of the data elements from each of the operational systems for easy analysis. Special programs allow the user to organize these data elements and run queries and analyses. Figure 8.4 shows this basic structure.

Building a data warehouse is a complex task requiring very special knowledge and skills. Foremost among these is how to structure all of these disparate data within the warehouse so that a query can be retrieved quickly. The wrong "architecture" can cause a query to take hours to run (or even crash the computer), while the correct architecture will enable the same query to run in a matter of seconds. But even beyond this, inevitably, data warehouse design issues amount to a trade-off between cost and functionality. Today, a small district can spend $30,000 or $125,000 for a functional data warehouse. The $30,000 model works well, with some queries taking perhaps fifteen seconds to run, while in the $125,000 version, that query will run in milliseconds. Thus, there is a trade-off that the district must choose between. (There are other differences between these systems, which are beyond the scope of this chapter.)

Data Warehouse Technology

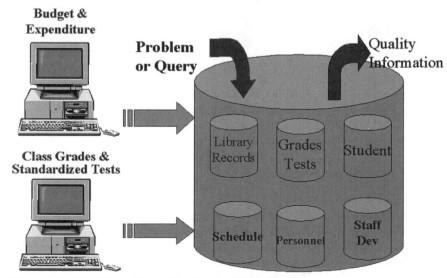

Figure 8.4   The Value of Data Warehousing Technology

All of this power and structure lies behind the scenes, just as a user of sophisticated word processing programs or spreadsheet programs is unaware of the thousands of lines of programming code necessary to make the program work. For example, I am writing this text using a common word processing program and a presentation program; however, I have no idea how the program was written, nor do I need or want to know. Further, I would never attempt to write a program as complex as this, even if I possessed some programming skills. Yet school districts sometimes hire staff or consultants to build relational databases using off the shelf programs. These attempts are largely unsuccessful in the long run because the challenge of building a three-dimensional (time versus data elements) data warehouse is far more complex than building a simple relational database (absent the element of time). Moreover, the process of data extraction from the source program and migration to the data warehouse can be a very complex process in and of itself. No doubt building a data warehouse for education is just as complex as the most complex warehouses used in the financial services or health services industries (as shown in Figure 8.1). What is important to realize is that data warehousing is a specialized skill requiring highly specialized programming skills. Educators cannot "build" their own data warehouses, just as the executive would not build one for a corporation.

Until recently, data warehouses were used only in large school districts, but even here they were more a compilation of existing systems tied together with specialized computer codes. While these efforts resulted in data warehouses, frequently they required large MIS staffs to operate and generate the queries—a problem that still exists in most large school districts. New advancements in technology have enabled the design of highly sophisticated data warehouses that can be accessed on the World Wide Web with easy-to-use, but powerful, on-line analytical tools.

Trend Analyses and Data Disaggregation: Getting It Done

The examples covered in chapter 2 looked at student performance over time, hence they can be thought of as trend analyses. In chapter 3 we looked at data disaggregation for equity analyses. Trend analyses and data disaggregation are common techniques employed in the analysis of data for decision-making.[26–29] In the examples noted throughout our discussions, these techniques were used to add meaning to the raw data. For example, trend analyses were employed for the SAT problem to determine answers to the many of the questions posed. Data disaggregation was used to add meaning to the impact of course enrollments in math (equity among boys and girls), as the data were disaggregated by gender. Performing analyses like these presents serious challenges to the productivity and skills of most school leaders, as even the simple task of bringing all of these data together into one database for analysis is time-consuming and complicated in and of itself. Typically all of these data would have to be rekeyed into one database unless someone on staff had proficiency in data transformation and consolidation techniques using tools such as spreadsheet and database programs. In summary, the entire process of data extraction and loading or rekeying it into a new database for analysis takes a great deal of time, which is why these analyses are infrequently conducted. When they are performed, often a mystique arises around the power and importance of the results, let alone the people who conducted the data transformations and analyses.

However, trend analyses and data disaggregation can be conducted more regularly and lose their mystique in the emerging technological environment of IT. In a data warehousing environment, queries and analyses such as these take only minutes—not hours, days, or weeks. While tools like spreadsheet and statistics programs are still needed for the statistics, many reiterative analyses can be conducted in less time than it took to complete only one query/analysis in the environment we find ourselves today. Instead of reviewing a single trend, when using data warehouses we can quickly review the trend of trends as we consider what improvements should be put in place. And data disaggregation can then be used as a tool for data exploration rather than as the object of the analysis. When we attain this level, frequency, and regularity of analysis, the techniques and the tools we employ help move us beyond fad to a real source of power and understanding about these problems and their possible solutions. I argue in this book that most meaningful data-driven decision-making occurs at this point, not when single analyses are conducted or limited measures are analyzed.

Summary

Data warehousing and the use of powerful information technologies are only now emerging fields of practice in education. At this juncture their potential to drive reform and improvement has just begun to be explored. However, what is certain is that educators lack the sophisticated IT tools that have been taken for granted in business and industry for a decade or more. Moreover, if one accepts the notion that multidimensional thinking is truly limited in the current paper and pencil decision-making environment, we are left to wonder how much progress is possible using information technologies in solving tough educational problems in a highly complex, social environment. And we have yet to explore how sophisticated problem-solving techniques such as rule-based and case-based decision-making techniques[30] can help us better understand how educational programs should be modified to meet the needs of students. We also have yet to regularly apply sophisticated data reduction techniques (data mining technologies) to identify hidden patterns among the vast amounts of data contained in a district's operational systems.[31,32]

To date, our ability to analyze school problems has been limited, prohibiting us from understanding how the relationships hidden within a 4500×13 data cube coupled with a teacher's, principal's, or superintendent's considerable wisdom and experience can be brought to bear upon a problem. What is most intriguing is that we do not have to invent anything new here. All of this technology has been around for at least a decade. What *is* new is that it is now becoming affordable. Thus, I believe that emerging techniques and tools for improved data-driven decision-making have the power to unleash creative problem-solving and unlimited multidimensional thinking that have as yet gone unexplored.

Notes

1. Vasant Dhar and Roger Stein, *Seven Methods for Transforming Corporate Data into Business Intelligence* (Upper Saddle River, N.J.: Prentice Hall, 1997).

2. Barry G. Sheckley and Morris T. Keeton, *Improving Employee Development: Perspectives from Research and Practice* (Chicago, Ill.: Council for Adult and Experiential Learning, 1997).

3. Dhar and Stein, *Seven Methods*.

4. Max H. Bazerman, *Judgment in Managerial Decision Making* (New York: John Wiley & Sons, 1990).

5. Charles L. Smith Jr., *Computer-Supported Decision Making: Meeting the Decision Demands of Modern Organizations* (Greenwich, Conn.: Ablex Publishing Corporation, 1998).

6. Jerry Hirshberg, *The Creative Priority: Driving Innovative Business in the Real World* (New York: Harper Business, 1998), 212.

7. Dhar and Stein, *Seven Methods*.

8. Andyne, www.andyne.com, July 1998. Now Hummingbird, Corp. See www.hummingbird.com.

9. W. H. Inmon, *Building the Data Warehouse*, second edition (New York: John Wiley & Sons, 1996).

10. Inmon, *Building the Data Warehouse*.

11. Melissa A. Cook, *Building Enterprise Information Architectures: Reengineering Information Systems* (Upper Saddle River, N.J.: Prentice Hall, 1996).

12. Louis Rosenfeld and Peter Morville, *Information Architecture for the World Wide Web* (Sebastopol, Calif.: O'Reilly, 1998).

13. Alan R. Simon, *Data Warehousing for Dummies* (Foster City, Calif.: IDG Books Worldwide, 1997).

14. Jae K. Skim, Joel Siegel, and Robert Chi, *The Vest-Pocket Guide to Information Technology* (Paramus, N.J.: Prentice Hall, 1997).

15. Richard Saul Wurman, *Information Architects* (New York: Watson-Guptill Publication, 1997).

16. P. Streifer, "Data-Driven Decision-Making through Fast-Track Evaluation: What Is It and Why Do It?" Invited publication—*Schools in the Middle Journal* (A publication of the National Association of Secondary School Principals). September 1999.

17. P. Streifer, "Putting the 'Byte' in Educational Decision-Making." Commentary, *Ed Week* (March 1999).

18. Dhar and Stein, *Seven Methods.*

19. Smith, *Computer-Supported Decision Making.*

20. Simon, *Data Warehousing for Dummies.*

21. Skim, Siegel, and Chi, *The Vest-Pocket Guide.*

22. IBM, Data Management Customer Solutions and Success, Web site: http://www.ibm.com, 1997.

23. Stanford International Mars Program, Web site: http://www.leland.stanford.edu/group/Mars/index.html, December 3, 1997.

24. Inmon, *Building the Data Warehouse.*

25. Simon, *Data Warehousing for Dummies.*

26. Victoria L. Bernhardt, *Data Analysis for Comprehensive Schoolwide Improvement* (Larchmont, N.Y.: Eye on Education, 1998).

27. Dennis P. Doyle and Susan Pimentel, *Raising the Standard* (Thousand Oaks, Calif.: Corwin Press, 1997).

28. Ruth S. Johnson, *Setting Our Sights: Measuring Equity in School Change* (Los Angeles, Calif.: Achievement Council, 1996).

29. K. Levesque, D. Bradby, K. Rossi, and P. Teitelbaum, *At Your Fingertips: Using Everyday Data to Improve Schools* (Berkeley, Calif.: M & R Assoc., 1998).

30. Dhar and Stein, *Seven Methods.*

31. Dhar and Stein, *Seven Methods.*

32. IBM, Data Management.

Index

~

About the Author

Philip A. Streifer is an associate professor of educational leadership at the University of Connecticut, where he teaches courses in executive leadership and data-driven decision-making. He is also a doctoral advisor to several students. He researches how educational leadership and organizations improve in a data-driven decision-making environment, speaking and publishing nationally on the subject. He is also president of his own firm, EDsmart, Inc., which develops and delivers affordable information technologies to schools.

Dr. Streifer served as superintendent of schools in Avon, Connecicut, and Barrington, Rhode Island, before joining the University of Connecticut. He has also held building- and district-level leadership positions in several Connecticut and Rhode Island school districts. He holds a Ph.D. in educational administration from the University of Connecticut, a master's degree in school administration from Central Connecticut State University, and a bachelor's degree in music education from the Hartt School of the University of Hartford, Connecticut.

He is married to Janet, a music teacher in West Hartford, Connecticut, and together they have two children, Lauren and Jeremy. Lauren recently graduated from St. Mary's College in Maryland, is working on her master's degree, and is studying to be a biology teacher; Jeremy is attending Bates College, majoring in chemical engineering.